*Emily Post on
Weddings*

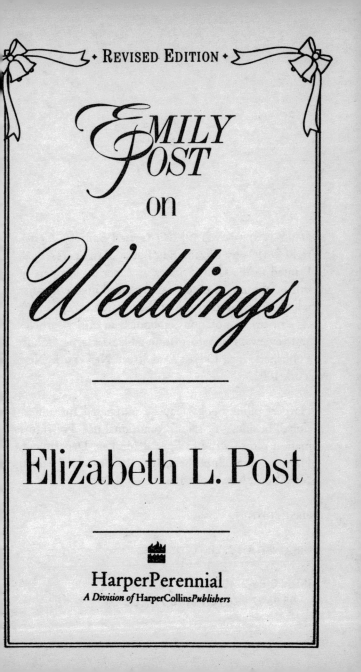

EMILY POST

on

Weddings

Elizabeth L. Post

HarperPerennial

A Division of HarperCollins*Publishers*

HarperCollins books may be purchased for educational, business, or sales promotional use. For information please write to Special Markets Department, HarperCollins Publishers, Inc., 10 East 53rd Street, New York, New York 10022.

FIRST EDITION

DESIGNED BY: C. LINDA DINGLER

ISBN 0-06-274008-3
    95 96 97 98 ❖/OPM 10 9 8 7 6 5 4 3

Contents

✦

Introduction

"My future stepdaughter is seven and her brother is nine. How can we involve them in our small wedding?" "My best friend is a man. I want him to be my 'maid of honor.' Is that all right?..."

These perplexing situations that brides of the 1990s are facing today are but two examples of the new issues that have become etiquette dilemmas for brides, their grooms and their families. Wedding etiquette, up until the past few years, appropriately dealt with questions about such topics as how to balance the ceremony seating when the bride had more guests than did the groom, and who danced with whom when at the reception. These are still important topics, and they still present quandaries to all involved in wedding planning. And they are still answered in this book because their answers are integral to successful, gracious and happy weddings. New to the book are numerous questions about situations that didn't exist before or that were so specific as to apply to only a few or that simply weren't addressed in traditional ways.

The future bride who already is living with her future husband is not a new scenario. But it is relatively new that it is a public one. No one is keeping her living arrangement a secret. Before, she would have been told to wear a nice blue suit for her wedding, which would be a small civil ceremony. Today, if she wants to wear a white wedding gown and have a formal ceremony and reception no one thinks it odd.

Would Emily Post approve of our new look at rules and guidelines that meet modern realities? I think so, for above all else she believed that, aside from those issues revolving around courtesy, thoughtfulness and consideration, etiquette had to be adaptable to the times. These can indeed be trying times for brides of any age, requiring flexible thinking and creative solutions. Recognizing that this is the case, this book has been completely reorganized to help today's busy bride find answers in a hurry. It presents solutions to every kind of question hundreds of brides have been asking me since this book was first published. I invite you to refer to the bride's timetable on page 19 as you begin to plan, and to use all the information on these pages that you need to ensure that your wedding is as beautiful and meaningful as you always dreamed it would be.

Elizabeth L. Post
1994

Engagement

Q. How do we tell our parents that we are engaged?
A. Your parents are the first to be told, but it is up to you and your fiancé whether you each want to tell your own parents privately or whether you go together to share the news. If your families are far away, you each should telephone or write your own parents. Although it may seem old-fashioned, it is courteous for the prospective groom to explain his plans to the bride's parents. This discussion is important evidence of respect for them. Today the bride participates in this conversation, possibly during the news-breaking visit.

Q. We've just become engaged. My mother is waiting for his mother to call and his mother is waiting for my mother to call her. Which family makes the first move to meet the other?
A. As soon as the prospective groom has talked with his parents, his mother should telephone your mother, tell her how happy she is about the engagement and suggest they get together. If your parents live far away from the groom's parents, a visit should be arranged between the families. Whichever parents can travel most conveniently should make the trip.

If, however, the groom's parents do not realize they should make the initial move, your parents should quickly do so. The only thing that's really important is that your families get together in a spirit of friendship.

Q. *My parents are divorced. Whom should my fiancé's parents call?*

A. The first call is made to the parent with whom you lived after the divorce or with whom you live now. If you also are close to your other parent, he or she should be called shortly thereafter.

Q. *My fiancé's parents are divorced. Which one of them should call my parents?*

A. The parent with whom your fiancé has been living, or with whom he lived after the divorce, is the one who makes the first move. If he lives alone, and neither his mother nor father has thought of contacting your parents, your parents should arrange to see his parents separately, usually meeting his mother first and his father shortly thereafter.

Q. *What should we do if one set of our parents disapproves of our engagement?*

A. You have a difficult decision. Either you assent to your parents' wishes, or you proceed with your plans to marry despite their disapproval. If you choose the latter course, you should inform them when your wedding will take place and that it would make you very happy if they would attend. In no case should you give your word that you will not marry if you really intend to do so.

Q. *May our engagement be announced before I receive an engagement ring?*

A. Yes. An engagement ring is not essential to

becoming engaged. If you have an engagement ring, you first wear it in public on the day of the official announcement of your engagement.

Q. *Does an engagement ring have to be a diamond?*
A. It doesn't have to be a diamond. A diamond is still the usual choice, but colored stones, semiprecious stones, or your or your fiancé's birthstone, have become popular in recent years.

Q. *Is my fiancé supposed to choose a ring by himself or may we select it together?*
A. You may select it together, certainly, but have an idea in mind as to what the budget is so that you are not looking at rings that are too expensive for the limits you have set or tinier or less expensive than your fiancé has decided he is able to spend because you are worried about spending too much. Communication is key here, and neither of you should be embarrassed about having a guideline to use for ring shopping.

Q. *How long should an engagement be?*
A. The ideal length of an engagement is between three and six months, unless there are reasons for a longer one, such as the need to finish college or a long term yet to be served in the armed forces.

Q. *Who gives an engagement party and when is it held?*
A. Once your and your fiancé's parents have met, an engagement party may be held. The bride's family usu-

ally gives the engagement party. If they cannot afford to do so or are deceased or perhaps live far away, the groom's family may give the party. The one requirement is that both you and your fiancé be present.

Q. Who makes the announcement at an engagement party?
A. There are innumerable ways of breaking the news at the party, from balloons or cocktail napkins with your names printed on them to a decorated cake, and there is not a rule in the world to hamper your own imagination. Since your mother, you and your fiancé should be standing at the door to greet the guests, there is really little need for an announcement at all! However, the conventional announcement is made by the father of the bride-to-be, in the form of a toast.

Q. How should a toast to the future bride and groom be worded?
A. There are many simple but lovely toasts the bride's father may propose, such as, "Now you know that the reason for this party is to announce Sarah's engagement to Hank. I would like to propose a toast to them both, wishing them many, many years of happiness." Another choice could be, "Please drink with me to the happiness of the couple who are so close to our hearts—Sarah and Hank." A very brief toast may be, "Will you all join me in a toast to Sarah and Hank."

Q. Does the bride or groom respond to an engagement party toast?
A. During the toast, both remain seated while everyone else rises and drinks a little of his or her beverage. The groom, at this point, should reply to his fiancée's father's toast. All he need say is, "Sarah and I want to thank you all for being here and for your good wishes." He may, of course, be more eloquent, if he wishes. The groom's father usually follows with a toast to the bride and her family. It is not necessary for guests of the party to propose toasts, but it is perfectly proper if they wish to do so.

Q. My fiancé lives in another city. May his parents give an engagement party to introduce me to their friends?
A. Unless the bride's family is unable to do so, they should not give an "official" engagement party. But they certainly may give a reception or a formal or informal party or dinner to offer you and their friends an opportunity to meet.

Q. Are gifts given at an engagement party?
A. Engagement gifts are not expected from friends and acquaintances. They usually are given only by relatives and very special friends, and they generally are given to the bride alone. Sometimes they are given by the groom's family as a special welcome to the bride. Examples of engagement gifts would be something personal, such as lingerie or jewelry, or something for the bride's linen trousseau—towels, a

blanket cover, table linen or a decorative pillow. Presents should not be taken to an engagement party. Since only close relatives and special friends give gifts, it can cause embarrassment to those who have not brought anything. If some guests do bring gifts, the bride should open them in private with only the donor present rather than making a display of them in front of those who did not bring anything.

In some localities and among many ethnic groups an engagement party isn't given to announce an engagement as much as it is given to celebrate the engagement. When this is the case in your family or among your neighbors, gifts are often brought to the party. A highlight of this type of engagement party is to end the evening by sharing the couple's excitement as they open the gifts.

Q. *Are written thank-you notes required for gifts given at an engagement party?*
A. If the gifts are delivered to you in person and you thank the givers sincerely at the time, you need do nothing more, although a note is always welcome. If you haven't opened them in the presence of the givers, however, or if they are delivered to your or your fiancé's home, you should write a note of thanks immediately. You should also write notes promptly in response to all welcoming or congratulatory messages that you receive.

Q. *Should we send printed engagement announcements?*

A. No, it is not in good taste to send engraved or printed announcements. You may, and should, however, send notes to or call relatives and close friends to inform them of your engagement before an engagement party or newspaper announcement. This prevents them from reading it first in the newspapers and consequently suffering hurt feelings. If your engagement is to be announced at a surprise party, you may ask them not to tell anyone else. Relatives who receive notes should telephone or write the bride as soon as they receive the news.

Q. When may I announce my engagement in the newspaper?
A. No sooner than the day after your engagement party, if you are having one. Otherwise, an announcement usually appears in the newspaper two or three months before the proposed date of the marriage. If the circumstances warrant, the announcement may appear up to a year before the wedding date, or as little as a week ahead. No announcement should ever be made, however, of an engagement in which either person is still legally married to someone else—no matter how imminent the divorce or annulment may be.

Q. Under what circumstances would it be in bad taste to announce an engagement in the newspaper?
A. The only time a public announcement is not appropriate is when there has recently been a death in either family or when a member of the immediate family is

desperately ill. In these cases the news is spread by word of mouth, although a public announcement may follow some weeks later.

Q. *My fiancé's family is from another town. Should an engagement announcement appear in his local paper? Should it be in his parents' name or in my parents' name?*
A. Your family should ask your fiancé's parents if they would like to have an announcement appear in their locality. If so, your mother should send the same announcement that will appear in your town's papers to the papers your fiancé's parents specify. The announcement of the engagement is always made in the name of the bride's parents or her immediate family. Even if the groom's mother puts the announcement in her local papers, she does so in the name of the bride's parents.

Q. *May we include a photograph of the two of us with our engagement announcement?*
A. Certainly, if the newspaper has space and its policy permits the inclusion of photographs. The photo used with an engagement announcement used to be of the bride alone, but today it is more and more frequently a photo of the couple. A black-and-white glossy print must accompany the written information you send the newspaper.

Q. *What is the general wording for an engagement announcement?*

A. Each newspaper has its own special wording, and many have forms for you to complete from which they write the announcement themselves. Send your announcement to the Society Editor one to two weeks before it is to run. The date on which you would like the news to be published should be given to all papers so that the notices will appear simultaneously. The usual form for your announcement is as follows:

Mr. and Mrs. James Welch of Mansfield, Pennsylvania, announce the engagement of their daughter, Amy Sue, to Mr. Arthur Ferguson, a son of Mr. and Mrs. Donald Francis Ferguson of River Forest, Illinois. A May wedding is planned.

Miss Welch graduated from Mansfield State University and is now Public Relations Director for Arista Records in New York City. Mr. Ferguson graduated from the University of Michigan. He is at present associated with HarperCollins Publishers, Inc., also in New York City.

Q. My mother passed away when I was quite young. My father wants to announce my engagement in the newspaper. Would my mother be mentioned in such an announcement?

A. Yes. When one of the bride's parents is deceased, the deceased parent is mentioned in the text of the announcement:

Mr. [Mrs.] Edward Patrick O'Mally announces the engagement of his [her] daughter, Miss Eileen Bailey

*O'Mally, to Dr. Francis Eagen . . . etc. Miss O'Mally
is also the daughter of the late Mary Smith O'Mally
[Edward Patrick O'Mally].. . .*

If one of the groom's parents is deceased the form
differs slightly:
*Mr. and Mrs. Richard Funck announce the engage-
ment of their daughter, Miss Alison Mary Funck, to
Mr. Robert Hagerty, son of Mrs. Francis Hagerty and
the late Mr. Hagerty. . . .*

Q. *My parents are divorced. In whose name is the
engagement announcement made?*
A. The mother of the bride usually announces the
engagement, but, as in the case of a deceased parent,
the name of the other parent must be included:
*Mrs. David Hillman announces the engagement of
her daughter, Miss Jillian Helmsley...Miss Helmsley is
also the daughter of Mr. George Helmsley of War-
renville Heights, Ohio. . . .*

When the divorced parents have remained friends,
and if their daughter's time is divided equally
between them, they may both wish to announce the
engagement:
*Mr. Glenn Besco of Philadelphia and Mrs. George
Carson of New York City announce the engagement
of their daughter, Miss Mary Ellen Besco. . . .*

Q. I have lived independently of my parents since college. How do I announce my own engagement?

A. Assuming you and your parents have maintained a friendly relationship, they still announce your engagement in their names. If you and they have severed all ties, however, you may announce your own engagement in the following way:

The engagement of Miss Lisa Jean Barth to Mr. John Tyler Gibson is announced. . . .

Q. How are second-time engagements announced?

A. Second-time engagements are announced by personal note or telephone call. If it is important to you to have an announcement appear in the newspaper, however, you include the same information that you included the first time.

Q. What happens when an engagement is broken?

A. The bride must immediately return her engagement ring and all other presents of any value her fiancé has given her. Gifts should also be returned with a short note of explanation:

Dear Hally,
I am sorry to have to tell you that Jim and I have broken our engagement. Therefore I am returning the tablecloth that you were so sweet to send me.

Love,
Lori

A notice reading, "The engagement of Miss Hally Cook and Mr. Henry Dobbs has been broken by mutual consent," may also be sent to the newspapers that announced the engagement.

If the groom dies before the wedding, the bride may keep any gifts she has received, if she wishes, as well as her engagement ring. If the ring is a family heirloom, however, and she knows the groom's parents would like it to remain with their family, she would be considerate to offer to return it.

Q. What should I call my fiancé(e)'s parents?
A. The question of names is a truly sensitive one for many people, and thoughtfulness must be observed on both sides. If you don't know your fiancé(e)'s parents well, you should continue to refer to them formally—Mr. and Mrs. Anderson—unless they specifically request you to use their first names or nicknames. If they do not bring up the subject and you feel uncomfortable, the best solution is an open discussion. If it seems too difficult a subject to bring up and a solution does not happen naturally, the safest compromise, during your engagement, is simply shortening "Mr. and Mrs. Anderson" to "Mr. and Mrs. A."

Q. I will be getting married after graduation. My fiancé and I attend different colleges. Must I refuse all offers to socialize this semester?
A. There is absolutely no need for you to sit home alone, but you should not have "twosome" dates, see

the same person frequently or let an occasional meeting with one person lead to others of a more intimate nature.

Q. *What exactly is a bridal registry and how should I use it?*
A. This is a service provided by many stores as a help to you and to your friends and relatives who wish to send a gift. You and your groom visit the stores in your area and select items you would like to have, including your china, silver and glassware patterns. The store opens a file just for you, listing the items you have chosen. When friends shop in a store at which you have registered, the personnel assist them by showing them the things you have chosen. If a purchase is made from among the items you have indicated, that item is checked off so another friend will not duplicate the gift. As a courtesy to friends of varying means, select items in a range of prices.

Q. *What is a trousseau?*
A. According to the derivation of the word, a trousseau was the "little *trousse*" or "bundle" that the bride carried with her to the house of her husband. There are no rules today about how much clothing you should have in your personal trousseau. It depends entirely on your financial situation and the life that you and your fiancé will be leading. If possible, you should plan to begin your marriage with a wardrobe sufficient to last you for one season, and preferably for one year, including the clothes

that are currently in your wardrobe. The three new articles that every bride should have if she can possibly afford them are her wedding dress, her going-away clothes and a nightgown and negligee for her honeymoon.

Planning Ahead

Q. *Can you give me a checklist to help organize the three months prior to the wedding?*
A. Yes. Keep the checklist in a convenient place where it can be referred to regularly and additions made or items crossed off as they are attended to.

At least Three Months ahead of the Wedding

____ Decide on the type of wedding and reception you want and the degree of formality and the size.

____ With your clergyman's cooperation, set the date and hour of the ceremony.

____ With your fiancé, make an appointment for a personal talk with your clergyman.

____ Select and reserve the site of the reception if it is not to be at home.

____ Choose attendants and ask them to serve.

____ Make out your guest list and ask the groom and his family to send their lists to you as soon as possible. Tell them how many guests they may invite, to stay within your limit. A card file is the most efficient system.

____ Order the invitations and announcements.

____ Order your bridal gown and those of your attendants.

____ Talk to the pastor, sexton and organist about music, decorations and procedure for the ceremony.

____ Engage the caterer if the reception is to be at home.

____ Engage the services of a florist.

_____ Make an appointment with a photographer for your formal wedding portraits, and reserve time for candid shots the day of the wedding.

_____ Engage the services of a videographer, if you plan to use one.

_____ If you plan to have live music at your reception, hire the orchestra or musician.

_____ Hire limousines, if necessary, for transporting the bridal party to the church and from the church to the reception.

_____ If the wedding is to be at home, make arrangements for repairs, painting and cleaning.

_____ If you wish, order notepaper for thank-you notes monogrammed with the initials of your maiden name and paper with the initials of your married name for later.

_____ Start to shop for your household trousseau and your personal trousseau.

_____ Select your china, crystal and silver patterns.

Two Months before the Wedding

_____ Notify your bridesmaids about their fittings and accessories. If possible, have shoes dyed in one lot.

_____ Select gifts for your bridesmaids and a gift for your groom if you intend to give him one.

_____ Go to local gift and department stores and list your choices in their bridal registries.

_____ At the time of, or soon after, the final fitting of your wedding dress, have the formal bridal photographs taken.

____ Make detailed plans with the caterer or manager of your club or hotel. This includes menu, seating arrangements, parking and so on.

____ Make medical and dental appointments, and be sure to make an appointment with your hairdresser for the day of your wedding or a day or two before.

____ Go apartment- or house-hunting with your groom.

____ Address and stuff wedding invitations when they arrive or obtain envelopes when ordering invitations and address them earlier.

____ Make housing arrangements for out-of-town attendants and guests.

The Last Month

____ Mail the invitations three to four weeks before the wedding.

____ Check with your groom about his blood test and the marriage license.

____ With your groom, select your wedding ring, and his if it is to be a double-ring ceremony.

____ Set up the tables for the display of wedding gifts.

____ Record all gifts and write thank-yous as they arrive.

____ Make a list of your honeymoon clothing and start setting it aside and packing as much as possible.

____ Check on all accessories for your wedding costume and also for those of your bridesmaids.

_____ Make final arrangements with the professionals who are working with you—florist, photographer, videographer, caterer.

_____ Change your name and address on all documents, such as driver's license and checking account.

_____ Check your luggage to be sure it is adequate and in good condition.

_____ See about a floater insurance policy to cover your wedding gifts—especially if you display them.

_____ Arrange for a bridesmaids' luncheon if you wish to give one.

_____ Address the announcements, enclose them in their envelopes and give them to your mother or a friend to mail the day after the wedding.

_____ Make arrangements for a place for the bridesmaids to dress. It is best if they are all together, whether in your home, at a friend's house or in a room in the church.

_____ Plan the seating of the bridal table and the parents' table at the reception, and make out place cards for them.

_____ Send your wedding announcement to the newspapers, with your wedding portrait if you wish. Large papers will send you their own form to be filled out.

The Day of the Wedding
In the morning:

_____ Have hair done or shampoo and set it yourself.

____ Pick up any orders that are not to be delivered—flowers, food, etc.

Two hours before ceremony:

____ Have bridesmaids arrive at your home to dress and to assist you with last-minute chores or emergencies.

One hour before:

____ Bathe and dress.

____ Ushers should arrive at church at least 45 minutes before ceremony to plan duties and seat early arrivals.

____ If you and your attendants are dressing at the church or synagogue, you should arrive now.

One half-hour before:

____ Groom and best man arrive at church.

____ Background music starts.

____ First guests arrive and are seated.

____ If you have dressed at home, you and attendants go to church and wait in private room or corner of vestibule.

____ Best man, on arrival, checks last-minute arrangements with clergyman and gives him his fee.

Fifteen minutes before:

____ Family members and honored guests (godparents, for example) arrive and are seated "behind the ribbon" or in the pews near the front.

____ The carpet is rolled down the aisle.

Five minutes before:

_____ The groom's mother and father arrive, and she is escorted in, followed by her husband (unless he is the best man). Finally, just before the music starts for the processional, the bride's mother is escorted to her seat in the front row, her husband takes his place beside the bride and the pew ribbons are put in place.

_____ The attendants take their places in the proper order for the processional.

_____ At precisely the time stated on the invitation, the music starts and the ushers lead the procession down the aisle.

Q. *What matters should be discussed with the minister or rabbi when we first meet with him or her?*
A. There are several points to cover, depending on your religion. A general checklist includes the following:

_____ Your preferred date and time of the wedding, and a time for the rehearsal.

_____ The service itself—whether it will be traditional and/or whether you wish to write your own vows or include special passages.

_____ Whether the minister or you should contact the sexton or organist about music, a visiting soloist or musician, etc.

_____ What kind of counseling the minister will have with you.

_____ What, if any, papers or documents the minister may need from you.

_____ Whether photographs or videotapes may be taken in the church before, during or after the service.

_____ Whether candles may be used.

_____ The minister's or rabbi's recommendations on the number of guests the church or synagogue will hold.

_____ Whether you or the minister should discuss such things as canopies, carpets, dressing facilities, candles, etc. with the sexton and what the charge will be for the use of these items.

_____ Whether there are dress restrictions for the wedding party.

_____ Whether the congregation will remain seated or stand during the procession and the service.

_____ Whether decorations are permitted, and, if so, when you or your florist can have access to decorate.

Q. May a relative who is a member of the clergy perform my wedding?
A. Yes, as long as your minister is willing. If he or she is, you and your fiancé should talk with both ministers or communicate by telephone or letter, as well as check as to whether the visiting minister wishes to make a preliminary visit to become acquainted with the church.

Q. We come from two different religious back-grounds. May my fiancé's minister be asked to partici-pate with my minister? How do we do this?

A. You must speak first to your minister to see if he or she is willing to weave components of both religions into your ceremony. If so, you then must speak to your fiancé's minister to see if he or she is equally willing. If both feel that they are able to work together and not violate the tenets of either religion, then you would meet with both of them to discuss details and your particular wishes. You might meet with each separately and then coordinate a meeting between the two of them, with you in attendance, to finalize plans.

Q. What expenses should we budget for when plan-ning a wedding?

A. First, list the categories of expenses you will be incurring and then obtain estimates from the vendors, services, etc. that you plan to use so that you have a realistic picture of the dollars and cents involved. The following list includes the basic expense categories for a large wedding. A smaller wedding may have fewer budget categories, so make adjustments on your own list accordingly. Try not to leave a single item out. For example, if you will have to lodge your atten-dants at a hotel, or provide a thank-you gift for a friend, relative or neighbor who will house your guests, be sure to include these as categories. Also include such things as shoes, gifts for your attendants and extra entertainment costs, possibly, for out-of-town guests. Although some of these items may seem incidental, the costs add up quickly and it is wise to prepare as comprehensive a budget as possible.

Invitations
Postage
Stationery for thank-you notes
Clergy fee
Sexton fee
Organist fee
Limousines
Photographer
Videographer
Flowers for ceremony
Flowers for parents, grandparents, etc.
Flowers for wedding party
Gifts for wedding party
Gifts for friends who help
Lodging for wedding party
Wedding dress
Shoes and accessories
Wedding cake
Reception costs
Music for reception

Q. What expenses do the bride and her family pay and what expenses do the groom and his family pay?
A. Before answering this question I must say that there are many variations not only in ways to save on wedding costs, but also in how the costs are divided. Today the bride and groom often pay their own wedding costs. The groom's family often offers to pay a

share and it is quite acceptable for the bride's parents to accept this offer. In short, the bride's parents are no longer obligated to pay for the entire wedding, but if they choose to do so they have the right to set the budget they are willing to spend; the couple and the groom's parents are also free to offer to pay any expenses which exceed the bride's parents' budget. Use the following just as a guide to what has been a traditional division of costs and make your own adjustments as necessary:

Traditional Expenses of the Bride and Her Family

> Services of a bridal consultant and/or a secretary
>
> Invitations, announcements and enclosures
>
> The bride's wedding dress and accessories
>
> Floral decorations for ceremony and reception, bridesmaids' flowers and bride's bouquet (in some areas given by groom)
>
> Formal wedding photographs and candid pictures
>
> Videotape recording of wedding
>
> Music for church and reception
>
> Transportation of bridal party to ceremony, and from ceremony to reception, if hired cars are used
>
> All expenses of reception
>
> Bride's presents to her attendants
>
> Bride's present to groom if she wishes to give him one

The groom's wedding ring

Rental of awning for ceremony entrance and carpet for aisle, if desired and if not provided by church

Fee for services performed by sexton

A traffic officer, if necessary

Transportation and lodging expenses for minister or rabbi if from another town and if invited to officiate by bride's family

Accommodations for bride's attendants, if required

Bridesmaids' luncheon, if one is given by the bride

Traditional Expenses of the Groom and His Family

Bride's engagement and wedding rings

Groom's present to his bride, if he wishes to give her one

Gifts for the groom's attendants

Accommodations for groom's attendants, if required

Boutonnieres for the groom's attendants

Ties and gloves for the groom's attendants, if not part of their clothing rental package

The bride's bouquet in areas where local custom requires it

The bride's going-away corsage

Corsages for immediate members of both families (unless the bride has included them in her florist's order)

The minister's or rabbi's fee or donation

Transportation and lodging expenses for the minister or rabbi if from another town and if invited to officiate by the groom's family

The marriage license

Transportation for the groom and best man to the ceremony

Expenses of the honeymoon

All costs of the rehearsal dinner, if one is held

Bachelor dinner, if he wishes to give one

Transportation and lodging expenses for groom's parents

Q. What expenses do the bridesmaids have?
A. The bride's honor attendants have the following expenses:

Purchase of apparel and all accessories

Transportation to and from the city or town where the wedding takes place

A contribution to a gift from all the bridesmaids to the bride

An individual gift to the couple

A shower and/or luncheon for the bride

Q. What expenses do the groom's attendants have?
A. The expenses of the ushers and best man are as follows:

Rental of wedding attire

Transportation to and from the location of the wedding

A contribution to a gift from all the groom's attendants to the groom

An individual gift to the couple

A bachelor dinner, if given by the groom's attendants

Q. *How much should the minister's fee be?*

A. Very often a minister or rabbi will have a set fee that includes pre-wedding counseling, the wedding rehearsal and the wedding itself. The best way to find out if this is the case is to ask. If the minister or rabbi does not have a set fee, then your donation gift to him for his services depends on the size of your wedding, beginning at anywhere from $50 for a small, private wedding to $100 to $300 for an elaborate one. If the fee is paid by check, it is made out to the minister unless he or she has informed you it should be made out to the church instead. If the minister has traveled a distance to perform the ceremony, both traveling and lodging expenses are paid for by the family at whose request the trip was made.

If the minister is a friend of the family or a relative, then he may refuse a fee. In this case, it would be appropriate to give him a personal gift. This gift can be something for his ministry or an item that supports an avocation or hobby, or luggage, desk accessories, a desk sculpture, etc. The list is endless, depending on the interests of the minister and how close you or your family are to him.

Q. *What questions should we ask when talking with the caterer?*
A.

Does the caterer offer a wedding package? If so, what does it contain and what does it cost?

Are substitutions permissible?

What food and drinks will be served at the cocktail hour and later in the reception?

Will brand-name liquors be served? If not, and you prefer that they are, what is the cost difference? May leftover liquor be returned and credited against the bill?

If you want an open bar for the cocktail hour and/or the reception, what is the cost?

What are the arrangements for champagne during the reception?

What does a sample place setting consist of?

Will you be able to observe a party arranged by the caterer before your reception?

Will the caterer provide the wedding cake if you decide not to use a bakery? Will you be able to sample a wedding cake beforehand, if so?

How many servers will there be?

Are gratuities included in the total package?

Will the caterer arrange for floral decorations if you are not ordering them from a florist? If so, does he have a book of floral arrangements from which to select?

If you choose not to have floral decorations

for the tables, are candelabra or other cen-
terpieces available?

Is insurance against china and crystal breakage
included in the costs stated? If not, is it
available and at what cost?

Is there an option to extend the reception an
extra hour? At what cost?

At what time do servers go on overtime pay?

Are there coat-check facilities and is there an
extra charge, if so?

How will tables and chairs be set up?

Do you have a choice of table linens?

Will the caterer provide printed directions to
the catering hall for you to include with
your invitations?

What is the deadline for your guest count?

Be absolutely sure that every service to be provided and
the total itemized costs are given to you in a contract.
Ask questions about any language you do not under-
stand. Read the contract carefully before you sign it.

**Q. When should we visit the florist and how do I
know who pays for which flowers?**
A. Flowers for the church, the reception and the
bridal party are ordered as soon as the details of your
wedding have been planned, including the date, type
and the colors of the bridesmaids' dresses.

In some areas it is customary for the groom to buy
the bride's bouquet. When this is done, the bride's
going-away corsage may form the center of her bou-

quet and it is removed before she throws the bouquet to her friends.

The groom provides the boutonnieres for all his attendants, the two fathers and himself, although the bride's mother often gives her husband his boutonniere, even though it may be ordered with all the others.

The bride traditionally provides the flowers for the church and the reception. Ask the florist if there is a wedding package. Be sure to ask, too, if there are extra delivery charges, and if these charges increase for deliveries to more than one location—such as to your home, the church and the reception site.

Q. What can be done with flowers from the church and reception after the wedding?

A. There are several thoughtful ways to share the flowers from your wedding. You may donate the ceremony flowers to the church, especially if your wedding is on a Saturday, for services the following day. If you plan to do this, be sure to consult with the clergyman or sexton so other flowers are not ordered for that day. You also may have the church and reception flowers delivered to a hospital or nursing home to be given to people who need cheering up. It is also thoughtful to send some of the flowers to a close friend or relative too ill to attend the wedding.

Q. When should we visit and select a photographer and what should we discuss?

A. You should reserve a photographer's time as soon as possible after you have confirmed the date, time and place of your ceremony and reception. In order to select a photographer, ask to see his or her portfolio and discuss the kinds of pictures you wish to have—both candid and formal. Your formal portrait is taken as soon as your wedding dress is ready—at least three weeks before the ceremony. This is especially important if you wish to have a picture of yourself in your bridal gown appear in the newspaper.

The candid photographs often begin with the bride's leaving the house before the wedding and continue through the day. You should discuss the schedule of the day with the photographer, how soon after the ceremony he or she may begin taking pictures (it is distracting and in poor taste to take pictures during the actual ceremony) based on your discussion with the clergyman, and when the formal pictures of the bridal party will be taken.

You should, of course, discuss cost and obtain a written estimate or contract once you have selected a photographer. Most charge a flat fee for the day and present you with the proofs to select those photographs you want printed at an additional charge per print. Others include an album with a certain number of prints included in the fee. Include the questions in the following list in your discussion.

> What does a wedding "package" consist of?
> What is the cost for additions?
> How many photographs will be taken?
> What is the number of pages in the photographer's standard wedding album?

What does it cost per extra album page?
What is the size and cost of extra albums?
What is the cost of keeping proofs?

If the photographer begins working at your home, covers the ceremony and continues through the cutting of the cake at your reception you should expect to feed him or her and any assistant he or she may have. They need not be offered every course from fruit cup to dessert but they should be offered the main course plus something to drink. Be sure to check this cost with your caterer before discussing it with the photographer.

Q. Does my family give a wedding album to the groom's family or should they order pictures themselves? What about pictures for my attendants?
A. Your family may give the groom's parents an album if they wish to, but it is not expected. More generally, the groom's family are shown the proofs and select as many photographs as they would like. The bride's mother places their order, but the bill is sent to the groom's parents. Your attendants may also order and pay for pictures they would like to have. You may, of course, select and order a picture of your attendants and give it to them as a memento, but it is not expected that you do so.

Q. We want our wedding and reception videotaped. Are there any guidelines on how to find and work with a videographer?
A. If you've seen videos of family or friend's weddings

that you thought were well done, ask for the name of their videographer. Contact several video studios and make appointments to see videotapes of weddings they have covered. Look carefully not only at the actual quality of the tape, but also at how it has been edited. Is the editing smooth or are there bumps, dark portions and gaps? Is the sound clear? Does it cover the things you would want covered at your ceremony and reception? Ask questions before signing a contract and make comparisons since prices vary widely.

Q. *When and how should we select musicians for the reception?*
A. As soon as you set your wedding date you should hire the musicians, since many are reserved months in advance. The size and formality of your wedding determines the type of music at the reception. It may be provided by anything from a CD player to a ten-piece band. At some very formal weddings there are two orchestras so there is continuous music. At other receptions, a strolling accordionist, guitarist or pianist provides the background music. The choice is yours, keeping in mind the preferences of your guests and providing a balance of contemporary music and slower, softer tunes.

These are considerations when you are selecting musicians. If you do not know of any, the caterer is often able to make recommendations. You also may check the Yellow Pages of the telephone directory and ask friends for referrals. Usually, a group in which you are interested will be able to give you a schedule of other appearances they are making so you can listen to them before making your choice. If possible try to hear the musicians play at a wedding reception similar in size and formality to your own.

As you make your selection, discuss the length of the reception, their price, the cost of overtime should you wish to extend the reception, specific songs you would like played and the number and length of the breaks they will take. As with your photographer, the musicians should be fed if you are having a lengthy reception, and this is something you should discuss with your caterer as well.

Q. We selected our wedding rings when we picked out the engagement ring. In what order are our initials engraved? Are both rings engraved the same way?
A. You really may engrave your rings with whatever sentiment you wish or just with initials. Today, most wedding rings are engraved with the initials of the bride and groom and the date of the wedding. When Elizabeth Ann Vitanza marries Charles Evan Northshield, they may choose to engrave their rings "C.E.N. to E.A.V." on his to her, or "C.E.N. & E.A.V." or with both sets of initials and a decorative symbol between them.

Although engagement rings are not usually engraved they certainly may be, if you wish, in any manner you like.

Your Attendants

Q. *When are the attendants invited to be in the bridal party?*
A. As soon as you have set your wedding date, you should invite your attendants to serve as members of your bridal party. This can be done in person, by telephone or by letter.

Q. *Is there any rule about how many ushers and bridesmaids there should be?*
A. The only rule is really a practical rule of thumb—that there be one usher for every fifty guests. Otherwise, the average formal or semiformal wedding party includes four to six bridesmaids and at least that many ushers. There may be more ushers than bridesmaids, but there should not be more bridesmaids than ushers. A bride need not have any bridesmaids but she must have one attendant or maid of honor.

Q. *May I have both a maid and a matron of honor?*
A. Certainly. If you feel you want to have both, your maid of honor takes precedence, holding your bouquet, being in charge of the groom's ring and serving as a witness. If you have both, you need to decide whether you then wish to have an extra usher to escort the matron of honor.

Q. *I can't choose between my two best friends. May I have two maids of honor?*
A. No, there is only one maid of honor. It might be easiest and eliminate hurt feelings if you simply tell

them both how you feel and flip a coin or draw straws to make your choice.

Q. My best friend is a man. I want him to be my "maid of honor." Is this all right? What should he be called?

A. I know that there are some who will tell you that this is the modern age trend in weddings and that it is perfectly all right. I do not think it is all right at all. Your maid of honor has many responsibilities to perform that may be difficult or awkward for a man to handle, no matter how close a friend he is. Your maid of honor stays with you and helps you dress before the wedding; she may assist with fitting schedules and arrangements with the bridesmaids; she helps plan or organize a shower or luncheon for you; and she helps you change into your going-away clothes. She holds your bouquet during the ceremony, helps you with your train and veil, and checks your makeup, hair and other personal details just before the ceremony.

If you have no female friends, then you might want to just have witnesses to your marriage, in which case they may be of either gender since their only responsibility is to sign a certificate stating that they witnessed your marriage.

Q. My husband's best friend is a woman. Can she be his "best man"? My sister is my maid of honor and my friends from school are my bridesmaids, so I really can't include her as one of my attendants. What should she be called? What would she wear?

A. I feel the same way about female "best men" as I do about male "maids of honor." If you are having a wedding, there is a bit of the traditionalist in you. Much of the etiquette surrounding weddings is tradition, and some of the traditions are definitely gender oriented. A best man has many organizational responsibilities for the groom. He also may stay with him the night before the wedding, throw him a bachelor party and help him dress and undress after the reception. If your groom-to-be has no close male relatives or friends, then it is likely he also has no choices for ushers. You might want to consider forgoing a traditional wedding and having a simple ceremony with your groom's best friend serving as a witness.

Q. *Is it obligatory for me to have my fiancé's sisters as my bridesmaids?*
A. No, it is not obligatory, but it is customary. If you have a problem in including them, be sure you and your groom-to-be discuss how you will handle the issue so there are as few hurt feelings or misunderstandings as possible. If they are much older and really not suitable "maids," perhaps you can include them in another aspect of your wedding or reception, helping introduce people or serving in another way.

Q. *What are the responsibilities of the maid of honor?*
A. In addition to holding your bouquet and the groom's ring during the ceremony and serving as a witness, the maid of honor is the bride's aide and

"consultant," relieving the bride of as many chores as she can, especially on the wedding day. Although it is not obligatory, a maid of honor who is not a member of the bride's family usually arranges for or gives a shower for the bride, often with the help of the bridesmaids. She is also in charge of choosing the gift that will be given to the bride from all the bridesmaids together, and collecting the money to pay for it. At the end of the ceremony, the maid of honor helps the bride adjust her train and veil when she turns to recess. She also stands in the receiving line, may or may not propose a toast to the bride and groom and she helps the bride change into her going-away clothes. The maid of honor also helps the bride's mother put away the bride's dress when the bride is changing to leave the reception.

Q. What responsibilities does the best man have?
A. At some point before the wedding, the best man consults the ushers about a gift for the groom and is then responsible for ordering it and collecting money from the ushers to pay for it. He also makes the presentation to the groom, usually at the rehearsal dinner or at the bachelor dinner, if there is one.

The best man also assists the groom in coordinating the clothing the ushers will wear. If it is rented formal wear, he helps the groom make sure the measurements and sizes are given to the store in plenty of time, that the ushers are fitted, if possible, and that the ushers are able to pick up their clothing. After the wedding, he takes care of returning the groom's clothing, if rented, and he or the head usher do the same for all the ushers' clothing.

The best man may help the groom pack for his honeymoon and makes sure that the clothes the groom will change into after the wedding are packed in a separate bag and taken to where the reception will be held.

He makes sure the groom is properly dressed in plenty of time and that he gets to the church on time. The best man is also responsible for the wedding ring and must make sure to get the minister's fee from the groom, which he delivers on behalf of the groom. He may do this before the ceremony while they are waiting to enter the church or, if he has time, immediately after the recessional. He sees the bride and groom into their car or, if there is no chauffeur, the best man drives the bride and groom to the reception himself.

At the reception, the best man does not stand in the receiving line, but mingles with the guests and helps the bride's family in any way he can. He is responsible for making the first toast to the newlyweds. After the toast, he reads aloud any telegrams or messages that have been received and keeps them carefully, to deliver to the bride's parents. The best man is the fourth man to dance with the bride after she has danced with the groom, the groom's father and her own father.

Toward the end of the reception he helps the groom change and makes sure he has everything he needs for his wedding trip. He then escorts the groom's family to the room where the groom is dressing, for their farewells. The best man is in charge of whatever transportation the bride and groom will use to leave the reception, and he keeps these plans secret to avoid the pranks of practical jokers. If the couple is leaving by car, he sees that their luggage is in the car and may either drive the bride and groom to their car or arrange to have it delivered at the moment of their departure. When the bride and groom are ready to leave, the best man leads them through the waiting guests to the door.

Q. Why doesn't the best man walk in the processional?
A. In Orthodox and Conservative Jewish ceremonies the best man does precede the groom in the wedding procession, because the groom is part of the procession. In Christian ceremonies the best man also stays with the groom, but since the groom is not part of the processional, the two enter the church through a door near the altar and the best man stays at the groom's side during the entire ceremony.

Q. What are the responsibilities of the bridesmaids?
A. Bridesmaids may be single or married contemporaries of the bride whose special duties include forming the bridal procession and, if the bride desires, standing with her in the receiving line. Later they circulate among the guests, acting as "deputy hostesses." Any of them may give a shower, or they may all give one together. Often, bridesmaids give a luncheon for the bride or attend one given by her. Generally they

give her a joint present, engraved with their names or initials, as well as personal wedding gifts.

Q. *What are the age limits for flower girls, ring bearers, junior ushers and junior bridesmaids?*
A. Flower girls and ring bearers are usually between three and seven years old. Junior ushers and bridesmaids generally are between seven and fourteen, when they are too big to be flower girls and ring bearers, but too young to be bridesmaids and ushers. Depending on their size and your wishes, they may be slightly younger or older.

Q. *What are the responsibilities of younger attendants?*
A. Flower girls used to scatter flower petals before the bride, but more often today they simply carry a basket or bouquet of flowers. A flower girl must be part of the rehearsal, but whether she is included in showers and the rehearsal dinner depends on her age and the wishes of her parents. Her dress is paid for by her family.

A ring bearer carries the ring or rings, fastened to a firm white velvet or satin cushion with a white thread or a hat pin. Often, facsimiles are on the cushion, and the best man and maid of honor carry the real rings. Like the flower girl, the ring bearer must attend the rehearsal, but his attendance at other functions is optional.

Junior ushers, if there are two of them, often are appointed to be in charge of the white carpet or the pew ribbons. Otherwise, their only duties are to attend the rehearsal and to be part of the processional and recessional. They walk behind the regular ushers and dress like them.

Junior bridesmaids, like junior ushers, are responsible only to walk in the procession. They attend the rehearsal, but they are not expected to give showers or contribute to the bride's gift. Junior bridesmaids need not stand in the receiving line, but may do so if asked to by the bride. Their attendance at the rehearsal dinner and at showers is not mandatory and depends on their age.

Q. What are the responsibilities of the ushers?
A. Usually the groom chooses one usher who is particularly reliable or experienced to be the head usher. He is responsible for seeing that the others arrive at the rehearsal and the church on time, assigning them to certain aisles and designating the ones who will escort the immediate family. The head usher may escort the bride's and/or the groom's mothers in and out of the church unless there are brothers of the bride or groom who are ushers, in which cases they would escort their own mothers.

The ushers see that all guests and family members are seated, insofar as possible, where they wish to be. Traditionally, ushers offer their arm to women they are escorting and the women's husbands or escorts walk behind. They do not offer their arm to male guests but do walk beside them to show them to their seats. An alternative manner is to have the usher lead a husband and wife or other couple, walking together, to their pew, and "usher" them both into it. Instead of offering his arm to the woman as a couple arrives, the usher simply looks at both of them and says, "Please follow me."

Two ushers are appointed to put the pew ribbons in position, and two others to lay the carpet (unless junior ushers are handling this task). Ushers attend the bachelor dinner, if there is one, or sometimes arrange it themselves, and they are expected to contribute to a gift for the groom.

Q. Do the ushers stand in the receiving line?
A. No, they do not. They should mingle with the guests while the receiving line is in place, and are seated at the bridal table, if there is one.

Q. What do we do if one of the attendants backs out right before the wedding?
A. You may, even up to the last day or two, ask another close friend to fill in. Friends should not be offended by a late invitation but rather ought to feel flattered that you feel close enough to count on them in an emergency. It would be most courteous of you to absorb any expense they will need to incur to participate in your wedding, however, since the cost would not have been planned in their budget. If there is no other friend available to step in, simply proceed with your wedding plans with one less attendant. If this causes awkwardness in your processional or recessional, ask your minister for advice on alternative ways to enter and exit.

Q. My future stepdaughter is seven and her brother is nine. How can we involve them in our small wedding? We want them to be a part of it.

A. Even though your wedding is small, you could consider asking them to be a junior bridesmaid and a junior usher, which would allow them to be with you both throughout the entire service and would undoubtedly make them feel very special.

Q. We can't have all our closest friends and brothers and sisters in our wedding party. Are there other ways to let them know they are special to us and have them involved?

A. Unless you have invited hundreds of people to your wedding, they will know they are special to you because they are included among those with whom you wish to share your special day. If there are one or two to whom you feel particularly close, you might consider asking them to read a verse or passage during your ceremony, or asking them to help make sure everyone at your reception is comfortable and happy. You could ask two friends to take care of a guest book, making sure everyone has signed it, as well. If there is room at your bridal table, if you have one at your reception, you could ask those close to you to sit at this table with you.

Invitations
& Announcements

Q. How far in advance of the wedding are invitations sent?
A. Approximately ten days to three weeks for an informal wedding and four to six weeks for a formal one.

Q. When should invitations be ordered?
A. As soon as you have confirmed dates and times for both the ceremony and the reception.

Q. What is the traditional style of an invitation?
A. Traditional invitations are engraved or thermographed on the first page of a double sheet of ivory, white or soft cream heavy paper. The paper may be flat or have a raised margin (called a plate mark or panel). Separate invitations to the reception are engraved on small, stiff cards appropriate in size to the size of the wedding ceremony invitation.

Q. What is the traditional wording and spelling for a wedding invitation?
A. Some of the specific rules for formal wedding invitations are as follows:

> The invitation to the wedding ceremony reads: "requests the honour (spelled with a u) of your presence. . . "

> The invitation to the reception, when not an enclosed card saying "reception following the ceremony," reads: "requests the pleasure of your company. . . ."

Invitations to a Roman Catholic ceremony may replace the phrase "at the marriage of" with "at the marriage in Christ of." They may also add, beneath the groom's name, "and your participation in the offering of the nuptial mass."

If the invitation includes the handwritten name of the recipient, the full name must be written out. The use of an initial—"Mr. and Mrs. James B. Simpson"—is not correct.

No punctuation is used except after abbreviations, such as "Mr.," "Mrs.," etc., or when phrases requiring separation occur in the same line, as in the date.

Numbers and dates are spelled out, but long numbers in the street address may be written in numerals.

Half hours are written as "half after four," never "half past four" or "4:30 p.m." or "four-thirty p.m."

"Doctor" is written in full, but "Mr." is never written "Mister." "Junior" may be written in full, although "Jr." is preferred.

No words are capitalized except those that would be ordinarily, such as people's names and titles, place names and names of the day and month.

The year does not have to be included on wedding invitations, but usually is on announcements since they may be sent long after the wedding takes place.

The invitation to the wedding ceremony alone does not include an R.S.V.P.

On the reception invitation, "R.s.v.p.," "R.S.V.P." and "The favour of a reply is requested" are equally correct. If the address to which the reply is sent differs from that which appears in the invitation, it is also correct to use "kindly send reply to," followed by the correct address.

Q. Should the style of the invitation match the formality of the wedding?
A. Yes. All the elements of your wedding should be consistent for a smooth and harmonious atmosphere. The invitations set the tone of the ceremony. If you have decided upon a traditional wedding you should use the formal, third-person-style invitation. If you are being married on a beach at dawn with a buffet breakfast to follow, your invitations might be a poem illustrated with shells.

Q. What is the correct form for an invitation to the wedding ceremony only?
A. The most formal wedding invitation, no longer seen today, had the name of the recipient written by hand. The most correct and more commonly used

form is:

> Doctor and Mrs. John Huntington Smith
> request the honour of your presence
> at the marriage of their daughter
> Millicent Jane
> to
> Mr. James Edward Pope
> Saturday, the first of November
> at twelve o'clock
> St. John's Church

R.S.V.P.

Q. *What is the correct form for a single invitation to both the wedding ceremony and the reception?*
A. The card described above may be used when every guest is invited to the reception, but it is more common and less expensive to issue a combined invitation:

> Mr. and Mrs. Joseph Gordon
> request the honour of your presence
> at the marriage of their daughter
> Anne Marie
> to
> Mr. David Mahoney, Junior
> Saturday, the twelfth of June
> at three o'clock
> Church of the Resurrection
> Ridgemont, New York
> and afterward at the reception
> Two Springdale Lane

R.S.V.P.

Q. *We are having a private wedding ceremony with only immediate family present, but would still like to have a reception for family and friends. How would invitations to the reception be worded?*

A.

> *Mr. and Mrs. Jason Gould*
> *request the pleasure of your company*
> *at the wedding reception*
> *of their daughter*
> *Susan*
> *and*
> *Mr. Sidney Abrams*
> *[etc.]*

Q. *How do we invite the few people we want at the ceremony?*
A. You invite them in person, by telephone or by handwritten note, explaining that you are having very few people at the ceremony, that it would mean the world to you to have them be among them, and that there will be many more later at the reception. You would send them the formal invitation to the reception, as well.

Q. *Our guest list for the ceremony is larger than for the reception. Do we need a separate invitation to the reception?*

A. Yes, in this case a separate reception card is enclosed with the invitation to the ceremony. The following example shows the most commonly used form.

Reception
Immediately following the Ceremony
Knolls Country Club
Lake Forest
The favour of a reply is requested
Lakeside Drive, Lake Forest, Illinois

Q. *How should a wedding invitation be worded when. . .*

. . . the groom's family gives the wedding?
A.

Mr. and Mrs. John Henry Pater
request the honour of your presence
at the marriage of
Miss Marie Dubois
to
their son
John Henry Pater, Junior
[etc.]

Q. *. . . the groom's family is co-hosting the wedding?*

A.

>*Mr. and Mrs. Thomas Coleman*
>*and*
>*Mr. and Mrs. Daniel Golden*
>*request the pleasure of your company*
>*at the marriage of*
>*Barbara Jill Coleman*
>*and*
>*Andrew Golden*
>*[etc.]*

Q. . . . *the bride has only one living parent?*
A.

>*Mrs. Albert Casseta*
>*requests the honour of your presence*
>*at the marriage of her daughter*
>*[etc.]*

or

>*Mr. Albert Casseta*
>*requests the honour of your presence*
>*at the marriage of his daughter*
>*[etc.]*

Q. . . . *the bride has a stepfather?*
A. If her own father has had no part in her life, and

her stepfather has brought her up, the invitation reads:

Mr. and Mrs. Bruce Denoyer
request the honour of your presence
at the marriage of their daughter
Francine Ann Colby
[etc.]

If the bride's mother has been widowed or divorced and has recently remarried, the invitation reads as follows.

Mr. and Mrs. Bruce Denoyer
request the honour of your presence
at the marriage of her daughter
[or, Mrs. Denoyer's daughter]
Francine Ann Colby
[etc.]

Q. . . . *the bride's mother and father are divorced and only the mother is giving the wedding?*
A.

Mrs. Virginia Barnes
requests the honour of your presence
at the marriage of her daughter
[etc.]

Q. . . . *the bride's divorced and remarried parents are giving the wedding together?*
A. The bride's mother's name appears first:

Mr. and Mrs. Paul Kassay
and
Mr. and Mrs. George Cook
request the honour of your presence
at the marriage of
Prudence Jean Cook
[etc.]

Q. . . . *the bride has no living family?*
A. If the wedding is given by friends, the invitation reads:

Mr. and Mrs. John Baxter
request the honour of your presence
at the marriage of
Miss Elizabeth Murray
to
Mr. Henry Fordham
[etc.]

If the bride and groom send out their own invitations, they would read:

The honour of your presence
is requested
at the marriage of
Miss Elizabeth Murray
to
Mr. Henry Fordham
[etc.]

or

> *Miss Elizabeth Murray*
> *and*
> *Mr. Henry Fordham*
> *request the honour of your presence*
> *at their marriage*
> *[etc.]*

The other possibility would be that the bridegroom's family would give the wedding, in which case the wording is the same as shown on page 58.

Q. . . . the bride is a young widow or divorcée?
A. Invitations may be sent by her parents exactly as were the invitations to her first marriage. The only difference is that both her maiden and married names are used:

> *Doctor and Mrs. Maynard Banks*
> *request the honour of your presence*
> *at the marriage of their daughter*
> *Priscilla Banks Loring*
> *[etc.]*

Q. . . . the groom is in the military?
A. If his rank is below Lieutenant Commander in the Navy or Coast Guard or below Major in the Army, Air Force or Marine Corps, his name is given this way:

> *Robert Armand*
> *Ensign, United States Navy*

Officers of the ranks stated above or higher have the title on the same line as their names and the service below:

Colonel Adam Manville
United States Air Force

In the case of reserve officers on active duty, the second line would read, "Army of the United States" or "United States Naval Reserve."

First and second lieutenants in the Army both use "Lieutenant" without the numeral.

A noncommissioned officer or enlisted man may have his rank and his branch of the service below his name or not, as he wishes:

John Philip Jones
United States Air Force

Q. . . . *the bride is in the military?*
A. A bride who is in the service usually does not use her title, although she may if she wishes to. The invitation would read:

Claire Mandel
Lieutenant, United States Army

Q. *My dad is deceased but I want to include his name on the invitation. How can I do this?*
A. You have to be sure that your invitation does not appear to be issued by your deceased father. Wording

could be:

> *Deborah Ellen Keyes*
> *daughter of Mary Ann Keyes and the late William*
> *Keyes*
> *and*
> *James Bryant Huseby*
> *son of Mr. and Mrs. Silas Jones Huseby*
> *request the honour of your presence*
> *at their marriage*
> *Tuesday the twenty-first of November*
> *[etc.]*

Q. *I am a medical doctor and my fiancé holds a Ph.D. Do we use our titles on our wedding invitations?*
A. Women use their titles only when the invitations are issued by themselves and their grooms. Holders of academic degrees do not use "Dr." unless they are always referred to that way.

Q. *My fiancé will receive his medical degree in June and we are getting married in July. Even though he won't officially be a doctor at the time that we order the invitations, should we use his title on the invitations?*
A. Yes, since he will be a doctor at the time of your wedding.

Q. *My sister and I are planning a double wedding. How do we word the invitation?*
A. With the elder sister's name given first, the correct form is:

Mr. and Mrs. Henry Smart
request the honour of your presence
at the marriage of their daughters
Cynthia Helen
to
Mr. Steven Bodow
and
Linda Caroline
to
Mr. Michael Scott Adams
Saturday, the tenth of May
at four o'clock
Trinity Church

R.S.V.P.

Q. *Our wedding will be held at a friend's home. Are the invitations issued in their names or in my parents' names?*
A. In your parents' names. The form would be:

Mr. and Mrs. Bronson Kelly
request the honour of your presence
at the marriage of their daughter
Erin Kristen
to
Doctor Kenneth O'Byrne
Saturday, the sixth of April
at eight o'clock
at the residence of Mr. and Mrs. Evan Hubert Dunn
East Lansing, Michigan

R.S.V.P.

Q. *My husband and I married in Europe three months ago and have just returned home. Our parents have graciously offered to give a wedding reception for us. How would the invitations be worded?*

A.

> Mr. and Mrs. Reid Michaels
> request the pleasure of your company
> at a reception
> in honor of
> Mr. and Mrs. Christopher Miller
> [etc.]

Or, a less formal invitation may be issued by using fill-in printed cards and writing "In honor of Melanie and Christopher" or "In honor of Mr. and Mrs. Christopher Miller" at the top.

Q. *What is the proper way to respond to a wedding invitation?*

A. Invitations to a marriage **ceremony** do not require an answer, unless the invitation has arrived in the form of a personal note. In that case it should be answered at once, also by handwritten note.

Invitations to the reception alone or to both the **ceremony and reception** follow the form of the invitation. If the invitation is in the traditional third-person form so is the response. The reply to a wedding invitation from Mr. and Mrs. Gregg Mariotti to Mr. and Mrs. William James DeRosa would read as follows.

Mr. and Mrs. William James DeRosa
accept with pleasure
Mr. and Mrs. Mariotti's
kind invitation for
Saturday, the first of June

or, if you prefer:
. . . the kind invitation of
Mr. and Mrs. Gregg Mariotti
for
Saturday, the first of June

In the event Mr. and Mrs. DeRosa could not attend the wedding, the phrasing would be "regret that they are unable to accept" in place of "accept with pleasure."

Replies to semiformal- or informal-style invitations do not need to be in the traditional third-person style. They may be answered by a short personal note, or even by telephone when that seems most appropriate. All invitations, no matter what the style, should be answered *as promptly as possible.*

Q. *Is it in good taste to enclose reply cards with invitations to a wedding reception?*
A. No, it is not. Unfortunately, however, many people today do not bother to answer a wedding invitation promptly by hand. The use of answer cards is sometimes the only way to determine accurately how

many people to expect. If you feel this is the case in your area, you are justified in using them.

Q. How can one tell invitees that their children are not included?
A. Since it is not correct to print "Please do not bring children" on an invitation, the best solution is word of mouth. If you are afraid your guests will bring them even though the envelope does not include their names, simply explain that you are terribly sorry but that you cannot include children. Ask those with whom you speak to help you spread the word.

Q. When the bride's parents are divorced and both have remarried, is it proper to include all four names on the invitation?
A. Only if both couples are sharing the expenses and acting as co-hosts. Otherwise, only the name of the couple who pays and acts as host at the wedding and reception should appear.

Q. My fiancé and I are giving our own wedding. May we still send out the invitation in our parents' name?
A. Yes, you may. It is perfectly proper and a lovely way to share the happiness of the event.

Q. Why aren't the names of the groom's mother and father included on the wedding invitation?
A. Unless the groom's parents are sharing the

expenses, your parents are the hosts and therefore the invitations are issued in their names.

Q. Why are tissues included in wedding invitations?
A. Engravers used to use tissue sheets to protect against blotting or smudging, but improved techniques have made the tissues unnecessary and you may discard them if you wish.

Q. I received an invitation with a small card that says "within the ribbon." What do I do with it?
A. This means that a certain number of pews have been reserved for special guests and that you are to be seated in one of these pews. Take this card to the church and show it to the usher who escorts you.

Q. What is an at-home card?
A. It is a card approximately four by two and one-half inches, slightly smaller than the reception card, that notifies your friends of your address after you are married. It is also an ideal way for the bride to let others know if she will be taking her husband's name or continuing to use her own name.

An at-home card may be included with the invitation or announcement and follows this form:

Laura Peterson and James Dennison
will be at home
after the thirtieth of September
323 Hinman Place
Mamaroneck, New York 10543

Q. Why are there often two envelopes for a wedding invitation?
A. The use of two envelopes is a tradition that probably goes back to when invitations were delivered by hand. For politeness the envelopes were left unsealed. Later, when mail services began, the unsealed envelopes were inserted into larger ones that could be sealed. A practical reason for using two envelopes today is that the names of family members, escorts of your invited guests and children can be listed on the inner envelope. However, today in the interests of economy and conservation it is perfectly acceptable to eliminate the inner envelope.

Q. When there are two envelopes, how are they addressed?
A. The inner envelope bears only the names of the people to whom the mailing envelope is addressed using neither first names nor addresses. For example, you would write "Mr. O'Donnell" or "Mr. and Mrs. Newberry."

Close relatives' inner envelopes may be addressed "Grandmother," "Aunt Julia and Uncle Edward," etc.

If you are including an invitation to an escort or date on an invitation to a single friend, the outer envelope is addressed to your friend and the inner envelope is addressed "Miss Richards and guest." If you know his name and address, it is preferable to send him his own invitation.

The outer envelope may include no abbreviations, either in the names or the street addresses. You may eliminate the middle name of the recipient, but if you use it, it must be written in full. For example, on the inner envelope you write only "Mr. and Mrs. Fulton"; on the outer envelope you write "Mr. and Mrs. William Andrew Fulton" or "Mr. and Mrs. William Fulton."

Q. How is the inner envelope inserted into the mailing envelope?
A. The invitation, folded edge first, is put in the inner envelope with the engraved side toward the flap. If the invitation requires a second fold, it should be folded with the engraving inside and inserted folded edge first.

If the invitation is folded twice, all insertions (such as a reception card) are placed inside the second fold with the printed side facing the envelope flap. If the invitation is not folded a second time, the cards are inserted in front of it with the reception card next to the invitation and any smaller cards in front of that.

The inner envelope, unsealed, is placed in the outer envelope with the flap away from you.

Q. My fiancé and I find traditional wedding invitations too formal for our tastes. Can we write our own invitations? If so, can you suggest the wording?
A. Yes, you may. Your invitation, in your own, less formal wording, may be engraved or thermographed

just as a traditional invitation is, or if your wedding is to be simple and untraditional, it may be printed on paper or a card with a design or border, often in a color carrying out the color scheme of the wedding itself.

Printers' wedding invitation books now include as many less traditional samples as they do traditional ones, so you might look at them for other ideas.

Two samples of invitations that seem warmer than the traditional form are included here. This one would be extended by the bride's parents:

Our joy will be more complete
if you will share in the marriage of our daughter
Susan Hall
to
Mr. James Bogard
on Saturday, the second of October
at half after four o'clock
6 Sesame Lane
Greens Lake, Pennsylvania
We invite you to worship with us
witness their vows and join us
for a reception following the ceremony
If you are unable to attend, we ask your
presence in thought and prayer
Mr. and Mrs. Hugo Stone
[or, Anne and Hugo Stone]

R.S.V.P.

Or, this invitation could be extended by the couple themselves:

Ellen Zimmerli and Gary Schatskey
invite you to celebrate their marriage
on Sunday, the nineteenth of September
at half past six o'clock
44 Beech Road, Essex, Montana

R.S.V.P

Q. *We are only inviting twenty people to our wedding. Would it be proper to send handwritten notes rather than printed invitations?*
A. Absolutely. In addition to the handwritten invitation above, another suggested wording might be:

Dear Aunt Sally,
Dick and I are to be married at Christ Church on November tenth at four o'clock. We hope you and Uncle Jim will come to the church, and afterward to the reception at Greentree Country Club.

With much love from both of us,
Jeanne

Q. *Just when may a wedding invitation be addressed to "Mr. and Mrs. John Smith and Family"?*
A. Only when every family member is intended to be included in the invitation. When the outer envelope is addressed in this way, the inner envelope is addressed "Mr. and Mrs. Smith" and (below) "Christine, Catherine and Robert."

Q. Are abbreviations used when addressing wedding invitation envelopes?
A. The only abbreviations should be Mr., Mrs., Dr., etc., never the street addresses or parts of names.

Q. At what age should children receive their own invitations?
A. Children over the age of ten should, if possible, receive their own invitations. If more than one child in a family is to be invited and you are sending one invitation for all of them, the inner envelope is addressed "Marion, Richard and Robert" and the outer envelope is addressed "The Messrs. and Miss Dowling" or "Miss Marion Dowling and The Messrs. Robert and Richard Dowling" below.

Q. Should wedding invitations have return addresses on the envelope?
A. Yes. Although in the past it was considered in bad taste, it now is required by the United States Postal Service that all first-class mail bear a return address. The return address may be engraved or printed on the back flap rather than on the front. Also, it is a way to provide a return address if no R.S.V.P. appears on the invitation.

Q. Should invitations be sent to. . .

. . . the person who performs the ceremony and his or her spouse?
A. Yes. It's courteous, and indicates that you definitely are including the spouse.

Q. . . . the fiancé(e) of the invited guest?
A. Yes. It's particularly nice to send him or her a separate invitation, but if that is not possible, his or her name should appear on the inner envelope below the name of the invited guest.

Q. . . . the bridal party members?
A. Yes. They are not expected to reply, but may like to have the invitation as a memento. A response card is not included.

Q. . . . the groom's parents?
A. Yes. It is a courtesy and also a special memento for them. Again, no response card is included.

Q. . . . relatives and friends living too far away to attend the wedding?
A. Yes, although many people prefer not to do this, feeling it might appear that they are merely asking for a gift. In this case they should receive an announcement or possibly an invitation to the church only, neither of which carries any obligation whatsoever.

Q. . . . small children who are not invited to the reception?
A. Yes, if it will be convenient for their parents to arrange to have them taken home before the reception—otherwise you may be creating an awkward problem.

Q. . . . *people in mourning?*
A. Yes, even though they may not attend.

Q. *Is it ever acceptable to invite one member of a married couple without inviting the spouse?*
A. No. Both members must be invited, even if you only know one of them.

Q. *May I invite only one member of an unmarried couple who are living together?*
A. No. Both should be invited. A single invitation should be sent addressed to Miss (or Ms.) Joan Morrison and Mr. Frederick Newsome on separate lines. In the event that you are unaware that your friend is living with someone and he or she asks if the other person may come after receiving your invitation, you should issue another invitation to the second person, if possible. If you have no more invitations, send a personal note explaining that you were unaware but would be delighted if both would attend.

Q. *Is it correct to invite co-workers in your office to your wedding with a single invitation posted on the bulletin board?*
A. Yes, so long as you are aware that it means that everyone and their spouses are invited. If you do this, it is a good idea to post an "R.S.V.P." sheet with it so you know how many people to expect. If you can afford the extra invitations, it is preferable to send them individually.

Q. *We've changed the date of our wedding. Our invitations have already been printed. Can we cross out the old date and insert the new one?*

A. Yes. If you have no time to enclose a printed card reading "The date of the wedding has been changed from May tenth to June sixteenth," you may neatly cross out the old date and write the new one beside it.

Q. *We canceled our wedding plans shortly after mailing the invitations. How do we inform people?*

A. There are three ways to do this. If you have time, a printed card may be sent:

Mr. and Mrs. Charles Markham

announce that the marriage of

their daughter

Denise

to

Mr. Pierce Delaney

will not take place

This method avoids your or your parents' having to answer questions when you are undoubtedly upset.

If time is short, invited guests must be notified by telephone and/or telegram. Telegrams would read "Regret to inform you wedding of Denise Markham and Pierce Delaney has been canceled." Or to closer friends, "Regret that Denise's and Pierce's wedding has been called off."

If you are relaying the message by telephone,

friends and relatives may be asked to help make the calls, thereby parrying questions so you and your parents don't have to repeatedly explain.

Q. *How do announcements differ from invitations? Who gets them and who doesn't?*
A. Announcements are just that—they announce that a wedding has taken place and they are sent after the wedding. It is never mandatory to send them, but they are useful. They place no obligation on the recipient to send a gift, but they serve to inform old friends who have been out of touch, business clients, people who live too far away to be able to attend and closer friends who cannot be included when the wedding and reception lists are small. Announcements are never sent to anyone who has received an invitation to the ceremony and/or the reception.

Q. *How is an announcement worded?*
A. The form of a wedding announcement resembles the form of the wedding invitation in everything except wording. The notepaper, style of engraving and manner of addressing the envelopes are all the same.

For many years the announcements were issued in the name of the bride's parents. I recommend that the family of the groom be included on the announcement with that of the bride as in the following example.

Mr. and Mrs. Howard Carter James
and
Mr. and Mrs. Stanley Homes Seaburn
announce the marriage of
Nancy Lynn James
and
Stanley Homes Seaburn, Jr.
Saturday, the second of May
One thousand nine hundred and ninety-five
Trinity Church
New Milford, Connecticut

R.S.V.P.

Q. *How soon after a wedding are announcements sent?*
A. As soon as possible after the wedding, preferably the next day. If there is some extenuating circumstance, they may, however, be mailed up to several months later.

Q. *What information should be included in a newspaper wedding announcement and when should it be sent?*
A. At least three weeks before the wedding, the announcement and the bride's photo should be sent to the newspapers and should appear the day following the ceremony.

Each paper will use as much information as it

wishes, and in its own words. Some large-city papers will return a form to be completed with all the information they require, but most will accept your copy.

In general, you should provide:

> Bride's name and address
> Her parents' names and their address
> Her grandparents' names
> Bridegroom's name and address
> His parents' names and their address
> Time of ceremony
> Place (church, synagogue, etc.)
> Location of reception
> Who will give the bride away—relationship to bride
> List of all the attendants
> Description of the clothing of the bride and her attendants
> Bride's schools
> Bride's profession
> Groom's schools
> Groom's profession
> Wedding trip
> Future residence

Prewedding Events

Q. *Who gives bridal showers and how many may a bride have?*
A. Bridal attendants, family friends, co-workers and relatives may give showers. Members of the immediate family—mothers, grandmothers and sisters of the bride or groom—should not do so. However, an exception could be made if all of the members of the bridal party are family members. There is no specific rule about the number of showers, but it is an imposition to ask friends to go to several and bring a gift to each. The bride should go over the guest lists with the hostesses and divide them so that no one person is invited to more than one or, at the most, two showers.

Q. *Are showers for women only?*
A. No indeed. Showers that include the groom and male guests are often held in the evening or on Sunday and I think it is nice that fathers and grooms can take part in the festivities. Certainly, it is fun for the groom, who is often not as much involved in the prewedding planning and festivities as the bride, to participate in a shower. The shower category, however, should be of interest to both the bride and the groom. Bottle or bar showers, workshop showers, garden and barbecue showers all are appropriate.

Q. *I'm being married for the second time. May my matron of honor have a shower for me?*
A. Yes, but it should be a small and intimate party

and, if possible, the guest list should be comprised of friends other than those who attended showers for your first marriage.

Q. *I have received a shower invitation that has a note saying "wishing well." What does that mean?*
A. This means that in addition to a regular gift, you have been asked to bring something for a "wishing well." "Wishing well" gifts are tiny presents—a spool of thread, a kitchen sponge, a wooden spoon, a can of soap powder, etc. The hostess usually makes a cardboard replica of a well and decorates it with paper, fabric, laces, doilies, ribbons, etc., and the gifts, wrapped and tied to ribbons, are tossed in. There are no cards on the presents, although at some showers the guests write a poem, which is wrapped around their gift. The bride pulls out the gifts with the ribbons and reads the poems aloud.

Q. *Must a bride write thank-you notes for shower presents?*
A. It is never incorrect, but it is necessary only for those guests who have sent a gift and are not present. If the bride personally and warmly thanks each friend for her gift as it is opened, she need do no more.

Q. *What is the bridesmaids' luncheon?*
A. The bridesmaids' luncheon may be given by the bridesmaids for the bride or vice versa. It is not a shower but rather an opportunity for the bride and

her attendants to have lunch together before the wedding. It is usually held on the weekend before the wedding so that those who are working can attend. The bridesmaids usually give the bride their joint present at that time and the bride may give her gifts to them.

Q. What is a bachelor's dinner?
A. It is a festive gathering of men to bid farewell to the groom's bachelor status and, as is the bridesmaids' luncheon, an opportunity for the groom and his attendants, plus other friends, if desired, to get together before the wedding. Toward the end of the dinner, the groom rises and proposes a toast "To my bride" and the men rise and drink the toast. Bachelor parties once were given by the groom's father, but that is rarely so today. Instead, the ushers usually arrange the party, or it may be hosted by fraternity brothers or co-workers.

Q. We will have a lot of out-of-town guests who will be arriving the day before our wedding and staying until the day after. Should we plan on entertaining them? What are our obligations?
A. Sometimes local friends will offer to host a barbecue, a luncheon, a cocktail party or just a home-base get-together for out-of-town guests. This is a nice addition to the visit for travelers, but it is not required. Usually, out-of-town guests will be staying at the same hotel or motel and will find each other, enjoy the opportunity to relax away from home,

swim in the pool or take advantage of sight-seeing in a new area. You are not obligated to entertain them, and you have no formal obligations to them. If you are so organized that you have time to entertain them, that is fine, but there are not expectations that you are providing a weekend's entertainment when guests accept your wedding invitation.

Q. When is the wedding rehearsal held? Who takes part in the rehearsal?
A. Usually it is held the evening before the wedding. It is attended by the bride, the groom, all the members of the wedding party and the bride's parents. The groom's parents do not need to attend but they certainly may, if they wish.

Q. Who gives the rehearsal dinner and who attends it?
A. The groom's parents usually give the rehearsal dinner, although it is not obligatory that they do so. If they do not, a member of the bride's family or a close friend may give the dinner.

The bridal party and their fiancé(e)s, spouses or live-in companions, family members of the bride and groom and, if possible, out-of-town friends who arrive the day before the wedding make up the guest list. The clergyman, if a family friend, and his or her spouse, is often included.

Q. Who sits where at the rehearsal dinner?
A. For a large dinner, a U-shaped table is ideal. The bride sits on the groom's right at the outside center

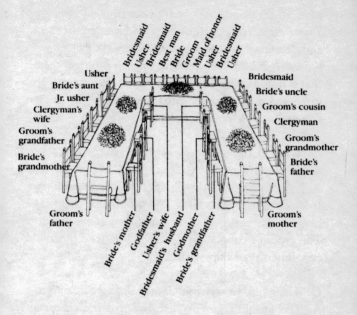

of the base of the U. Her maid of honor sits on the groom's left, his best man on the bride's right. The attendants sit on either side, alternating bridesmaids and ushers. The host and hostess sit at the two ends of the U. If they are the groom's parents, then the bride's mother sits on the groom's father's right and the bride's grandmother on his left. The bride's father sits on the groom's mother's right and the bride's grandfather sits on her left. The other guests are seated along both sides of the arm of the U, in whatever order seems the most congenial.

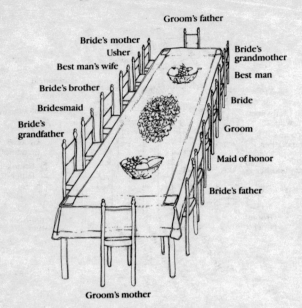

Groom's father

Bride's mother
Usher
Best man's wife
Bride's brother
Bridesmaid
Bride's grandfather

Bride's grandmother
Best man
Bride
Groom
Maid of honor
Bride's father

Groom's mother

At a smaller dinner a rectangular table is best. The bride and groom sit together at the center of the one long side, their attendants beside them, the host and hostess at either end and other guests in between.

Your Ceremony

Q. *My fiancé and I have been living together for three years. My mother says I can't have a formal wedding and wear a white gown. Is she right?*

A. Your mother would have been right a few decades ago, but times have changed and more and more couples are electing to live together before marriage. You may wear a white, ecru or ivory gown.

Q. *My fiancé was married before in a large, formal wedding. I've never been married and have always dreamed of a formal wedding. Since this is his second wedding, should we have just a simple ceremony, or may we have a formal wedding?*

A. You may plan as simple or as lavish a wedding as you wish. The fact that the groom has been married before does not prevent you from having a formal wedding.

Q. *After deciding the date and site of the wedding, are there any rules about choosing the hour of the ceremony?*

A. No, there really aren't any rules, although certain customs, climates and personal preferences are "rules of thumb." For example, Catholic weddings that include a nuptial mass were traditionally held at noon or earlier to accommodate those who fast before mass. Although this is no longer necessary, many Catholic weddings are still held at that hour. In the South, summer weddings are often held in the evening since the days are so warm. In the East, formal Protestant weddings most often are held at four or five o'clock in the afternoon. Whatever time you choose, it is best to plan the reception immediately following the wedding so that your out-of-town guests are not left wondering what to do or where to go.

Q. *Who decides the number of guests?*
A. This is determined by whoever is hosting the wedding reception, based, of course, on their budget and the number of guests who will fit comfortably in the planned accommodations.

Q. *How is the total number of invitations divided between the bride's family and the groom's?*
A. Invitations should be divided in half, especially if both families are of roughly equal size and if they live in the same community. Even if the groom's parents live in another community the offer of half of the invitations should be made. The groom's mother who will have an idea of how many of the groom's family and friends will travel to the wedding gives this information to the bride's mother. If this number is less than the number allotted to the groom's family, the bride's mother is free to issue this number of extra invitations.

Q. *The groom's mother wishes to invite more than the number of places allotted to the groom's family. How do we handle this situation?*
A. The size of a wedding reception is determined by choice and by financial necessity, or both, and the groom's mother should make every effort to stay

within the number of places allocated to her. Your mother should be frank, if asked to increase the size, and explain that either the planned size is what the space can accommodate, or that the planned size is what you can afford. If the groom's mother feels she must invite more than her allocated number and space is not the issue, then she and her husband should suggest that they pay a share of the expenses sufficient to cover the additional costs. If this is not satisfactory or if you and your parents do not want to alter your plans, she can plan a reception for you and your groom after your honeymoon, inviting the friends who could not be included at the wedding.

Q. I'm confused about what clothing should be worn by me, the wedding party and our guests for morning, afternoon and evening weddings. Are there any guidelines?
A. Yes, there are. Starting on the next page is a chart that will enable you to see at a glance the correct combination for every type of wedding.

Q. What should a bride who is being married for the second time wear?
A. She should not wear pure white, a veil, orange blossoms or a dress with a train. For a very simple wedding, a short cocktail dress or suit in a pastel color is always in good taste. For a more elaborate wedding, a long dress in a very pale color, off-white or white with color in the trim and in her accessories is lovely and most appropriate.

Most Formal Daytime

Bride	Long white dress, train and veil; gloves optional
Bride's attendants	Long dresses, matching shoes; gloves are bride's option
Groom, his attendants, bride's father	Cutaway coat, striped trousers, pearl gray waistcoat, white stiff shirt, turndown collar with gray-and-black-striped four-in-hand or wing collar with ascot, grey gloves, black silk socks, black kid shoes
Mothers of couple	Long or short dresses; hat, veil or hair ornament; gloves
Women guests	Street-length cocktail or afternoon dresses (colors are preferable to black or white); gloves; head covering optional
Men guests	Dark suits; conservative shirts and ties

Most Formal Evening	Semiformal Daytime
Same as most formal daytime	Long white dress; short veil and gloves optional
Same as most formal daytime	Same as most formal daytime
Black tailcoat and trousers, white pique waistcoat, starched-bosom shirt, wing collar, white bow tie, white gloves, black silk socks, black patent-leather shoes or pumps or black kid smooth-toe shoes	Black or charcoal sack coat, dove gray waist coat, white pleated shirt, starched turndown collar or soft white shirt with four-in-hand tie, gray gloves, black smooth-toe shoes
Usually long evening or dinner dress, dressy short cocktail permissible; veil or hair ornament if long dress; small hat, if short; gloves	Long or street-length dresses, gloves; head covering optional
Depending on local custom, long or short dresses; if long, veil or ornament—otherwise, hat optional; gloves	Short afternoon or cocktail dress; head covering for church optional
If women wear long dresses, tuxedos; if short dresses, dark suits	Dark suits

Semiformal
Evening

Bride	Same as semiformal daytime
Bride's attendants	Same length and degree of formality as bride's dress
Groom, his attendants, bride's father	Winter, black tuxedo; summer, white jacket; pleated or pique soft shirt, black cummerbund, black bow tie, no gloves, black patent-leather or kid shoes
Mothers of couple	Same as semiformal daytime
Women guests	Cocktail dresses, gloves; head covering for church optional
Men guests	Dark suits

Groom's father: He may wear the same costume as the groom and his attendants, especially if he is to stand in the receiving line. If he is not to take part and does not wish to dress formally, he may wear the same clothes as the men guests.

Informal Daytime	Informal Evening
Short afternoon dress, cocktail dress, or suit	Long dinner dress or short cocktail dress or suit
Same style as bride	Same style as bride
Winter, dark suit; summer, dark trousers with linen jacket or white trousers with navy or charcoal jacket; soft shirt, conservative four-in-hand tie; hot climate, white suit	Tuxedo if bride wears dinner dress; dark suit in winter, lighter suit in summer
Short afternoon or cocktail dresses	Same length dress as bride
Afternoon dresses, gloves; head covering for church optional	Afternoon or cocktail dresses, gloves; head covering for church optional
Dark suits; light trousers and dark blazers in summer	Dark suits

Q. *I have a three-year-old son. May I wear a white wedding gown at my forthcoming marriage?*
A. You should consider an off-white, pastel or white with color in the trim and accessories tea-length or shorter gown and wear flowers in your hair or a hat, not a veil.

Q. *Is the attire for the bridal party and guests the same for a Jewish wedding as for a Christian ceremony?*
A. Brides and attendants wear almost the same clothing as is worn for a Christian ceremony, although Orthodox brides are always veiled. At Conservative and Orthodox weddings all men must wear yarmulkes or, if the wedding attire is formal, top hats during the ceremony. They may be taken off after a Conservative wedding ceremony but must be worn during both the ceremony and the reception at Orthodox weddings.

Q. *Do men in the wedding party wear dinner jackets (tuxedos) at all formal weddings?*
A. No, tuxedos are worn only for semiformal and some informal evening weddings or a wedding after five in the afternoon when the reception will extend into the evening. See the chart on pages 94–97 for a list of appropriate clothing for the groom and his attendants.

Q. *My fiancé is in the military. Should he wear his uniform for our wedding?*

A. If it is important to him and you approve, he certainly may wear his uniform.

Q. Should my mother and my fiancé's mother wear the same length and style of dress?
A. It certainly looks attractive if both your mothers are dressed similarly, especially since they stand together in the receiving line. The bride's mother is the first to decide on what she will wear—how long her dress will be, what style and what color. She should then tell the groom's mother what her decision is so the latter may plan her costume accordingly. If the groom's mother feels uncomfortable in the type of clothing chosen by the bride's mother, however, she should be free to select something in which she will feel attractive and happy.

Whatever they choose, their dresses should not be the same color as your bridesmaids' dresses, nor should they both wear the same color, nor should they clash with each other or with the wedding party. Neither mother should wear black or white.

Q. What style of clothing should the fathers wear?
A. Although it is not obligatory, the father of the bride should dress in the same style as the groom and his attendants. Since he walks in the procession with the others, it presents a more unified picture if he dresses as they do.

The groom's father also may dress in the same fashion as the other men of the wedding party, especially if he is to stand in the receiving line. If he does not take part, however, and does not wish to dress formally, he may wear the same clothes as the male guests. See the chart on pages 94–97 for specifics. Both men wear boutonnieres.

Q. Do the maid and matron of honor dress differently than the bridesmaids?
A. The style of their dresses is the same, but the color may be a shade darker or lighter, or even in a different but complementary color family.

Q. What do flower girls, ring bearers, junior bridesmaids and junior ushers wear?
A. A flower girl's dress may be similar to the bridesmaids' dresses or it may be modified to a child's style, in a matching or blending color. In some areas, flower girls wear white dresses, preferably in the same white family as the bride's gown.

The most appropriate dress for a ring bearer is short pants and an Eton jacket, preferably white, but occasionally navy. Small versions of the ushers' apparel are not appropriate. Junior bridesmaids and junior ushers dress exactly like their senior counterparts.

Q. What flowers are appropriate for the bride and her attendants?
A. The flowers should be in keeping with the character and formality of the wedding and may be as simple as a single rose or as elaborate as a full cascade. Consult with your florist on such things as appropriateness, cost and seasonal considerations.

The bride's bouquet is almost always made up of white flowers, unless she is wearing a pastel dress or has been married before. In that case, the flowers would be of the same color or a shade that would complement her gown. White orchids, calla lilies, gardenias, stephanotis and lilies of the valley are among the most popular choices with an elegant white gown.

Be sure the style of the arrangement complements the style of your dress, and that the textures of both are complementary, too. For example, camellias and gardenias, with their shiny, dark leaves, are beautiful against a satin or brocade dress, while eyelet and cotton are better complemented by daisies or sweet peas.

The bride who is marrying for a second time may carry a simple bouquet, wear a corsage or carry flowers pinned to her purse or prayer book. They may be white or a color complementary to her ensemble.

When the bridesmaids' dresses are all of the same color, so are their bouquets. The maid of honor's may be of a different color, but the style should be the same.

Flower girls sometimes carry a little basket filled with rose petals which they strew in the bride's path. Others carry a tiny old-fashioned bouquet or a small basket of flowers.

The bride's attendants sometimes wear flowers in their hair, too, but they should be able to last the duration of the ceremony and reception without wilting or turning brown at the edges. This is the one place where silk flowers may be used, but they must be in keeping with the flowers they carry.

Q. *Are the boutonnieres the same for all men in the wedding party?*
A. No. The ushers almost always wear carnations. The best man and the fathers may wear white carnations, too, or they may be given a gardenia. The groom generally wears a different flower from those of the other men, such as a sprig or two of lily of the valley, a gardenia if the others are not wearing them or stephanotis.

Q. *What decorations can be used for a church wedding?*
A. Your decision really depends on several factors, such as the size and style of the church itself, the formality of your wedding, the cost and the regulations practiced by the clergyman or church.

A large church with high ceilings needs many tall floral arrangements to have them show up at all. Even in a small church, remember that the flowers are seen from some distance, and bolder flower varieties in simple, clear arrangements show up better than small blossoms.

Church flowers are generally white and, if possible, coordinated with the bride's flowers. This is not mandatory, however. They may also be of a color that blends with the dresses and flowers of the bridal attendants.

Many weddings have two arrangements of flowers on the altar and/or a spray on either side of the chancel steps. In addition, a cluster of flowers, a cascade of greens or a fall of flowers and ribbons may be used to decorate the ends of every pew, the reserved pews or merely the last of the reserved pews from which the ribbon will start.

Q. *How can we make our large church seem more intimate for our small wedding service?*

A. One effective decorating technique is to rent pots of shrubbery to form a "hedge" in front of the pews that will not be occupied. If the altar, chancel and occupied pews are brightly lighted and the area behind the screen of greens is left almost dark, the part of the church you are using will seem more intimate. Although your guests would use the aisle, the wedding party would enter from the vestry or waiting room rather than proceeding down the long, dark aisle.

Or, if there are choir stalls, use them as pews and have only the chancel lighted. This gives the smallest wedding all the solemn beauty of church surroundings but in a warm environment.

Q. *Our wedding and reception are going to be at home. How should we decorate?*

A. There are many variables, such as the size and shape of the room(s) to be used and the style of the wedding. In general, decorations consist of a screen or backdrop of greens or a dark drapery behind the improvised altar and vases of flowers in the windows, on newel posts and on occasional tables. If there is a fireplace, it may be filled with greens and the mantel decorated with green roping or an arrangement of greens and flowers. If you are having an altar rail, decorating it with greens and placing tall stands holding flower arrangements creates a lovely frame for the ceremony.

If you are serving refreshments in another room, table decorations may be either white or pastels that complement the bridesmaids' dresses and flowers.

Q. *What music is appropriate for a religious ceremony?*

A. There are many appropriate and lovely pieces from which to choose, including the traditional "Wedding March" by Wagner for a processional and Mendelssohn's "Wedding March" for a recessional. There are many other triumphal hymns and marches, and it is best to check with the organist to be sure they are approved by the church.

Background organ music played while your guests arrive at the church is customary. This is also a time when guest musicians—guitarists, flutists, etc.—play. Again, check your selections with the organist since most churches will not allow popular music. A selected list of appropriate music—also excellent choices for a soloist—might include:

> "Jesu Joy of Man's Desiring" by Bach
> "Ave Maria" by Schubert
> Chorale Prelude, "In Thee Is Joy" by Bach
> "The Lord's Prayer" by Malotte
> "Liebestraum" by Liszt
> "Biblical Songs" by Dvořák

"Joyful, Joyful, We Adore Thee" by Beethoven
"The King of Love My Shepherd Is" by
    Hinsworth

*Q. I'm close to both my father and my stepfather and
they are cordial to one another. Can they both walk
me up the aisle?*
A. No, they should not both walk you up the aisle.
The bride's father, by tradition, has the prerogative to
escort his daughter and he should not be asked to give
this up or to share the honor, no matter how cordial
the relationship with your stepfather.

*Q. This is my second wedding. Should my father
"give me away" or is that a little silly since I haven't
lived with my parents for years?*
A. Your father may escort you—no one really
"gives" the bride away anymore—or you may walk
alone, if you prefer.

Q. Who escorts the bride if she has no father?
A. A brother, uncle, godfather and close family friend
are all excellent choices. Although it is not at all traditional, the bride's mother may serve as escort if that is
what would make the bride the happiest. If there are
no suitable relatives or friends, it also is untraditional
but acceptable for the groom to escort the bride or
for the bride to walk alone. The determining factor is
the bride's wishes, after consultation with the clergyman.

Q. My parents are divorced and each has remarried. Where do my parents sit in the church?
A. The same procedure applies to both the bride's and the groom's parents, with the bride's parents' seating arrangement on the left side of the aisle and the groom's parents on the right side.

Your mother and stepfather sit in the front pew with members of your mother's immediate family—grandparents, aunts and uncles—immediately behind them. If your parents have remained on friendly terms, your father sits in the next pew back with his wife and their family members.

If your parents have not remained on friendly terms but you are close to both of them, it is more difficult. Your mother still sits in the front pew, but your father would sit two or three rows farther back. If you have been living with your father and step-mother and have had little to do with your own mother, your father and your stepmother sit in the front pew and your mother sits farther back.

Q. I was married before and am still close to my ex-husband's family. Would it be wrong to invite them to my wedding?
A. No, it would not be wrong, although, no matter how close you are, they may find it difficult to actually be at your wedding, which might represent a more final break than they have felt before. That choice is theirs, however, so if you want to invite them, go ahead and do so.

Q. Do friends of the bride always sit on one side of the church and friends of the groom on the other?
A. They usually do. The left side of the church is the bride's; the right side the groom's. At weddings where the great majority of guests are friends of one family or the other, the ushers may ask some of them if they would mind sitting on the other side. This not only makes the congregation look more balanced but offers more guests the desirable seats near the aisle.

Q. Does the mother of the bride (or groom) wear a coat as she walks up the aisle when the weather is cold?
A. No. As a rule, the mothers leave their outer wear in the vestibule of the church so as not to spoil the effect of their dress. If the church is cold, they may have their coats put in the pews by an usher ahead of time, to be thrown over their shoulders during the ceremony.

Q. Can anyone be seated after the bride's mother is escorted up the aisle?
A. No. If people arrive after that, they must stand in the vestibule, go to the balcony or slip into a rear pew from a side aisle.

Q. What is the order of attendants in the processional?
A. The ushers lead the procession, walking two by two, the shortest men first. Junior ushers follow the adults. Junior bridesmaids come next. The bridesmaids follow, usually walking in pairs also. When

there are very few bridesmaids or an uneven number, they may walk in single file. After the bridesmaids comes the matron of honor, then the maid of honor. A flower girl and finally the ring bearer immediately precede the bride and her father.

Q. Does the bride walk up the aisle on her father's right arm or left arm?
A. His right arm. When she and her father reach the groom, who is standing to the center right at the head of the aisle, she then will be next to him with her right arm free to be given to him. This also leaves the bride's father in the most convenient position to reach his seat in the left pew afterward.

Q. How long does the father remain at her side after the bride reaches the groom's side?
A. Until the clergyman says "Who giveth this woman to be married?" After answering, the bride's father turns and joins his wife in the pew.

Q. The phrase "giving the bride away" in the wedding ceremony makes me see red. Can you offer an alternative to including the question "Who gives this woman. . . ?" in the wedding ceremony?
A. If you feel so strongly about deleting this question from your wedding ceremony, by all means discuss your feelings with your clergyman. You may find him receptive to your objections and able to offer you an alternative you find acceptable. I know of one young woman whose clergyman replaced the

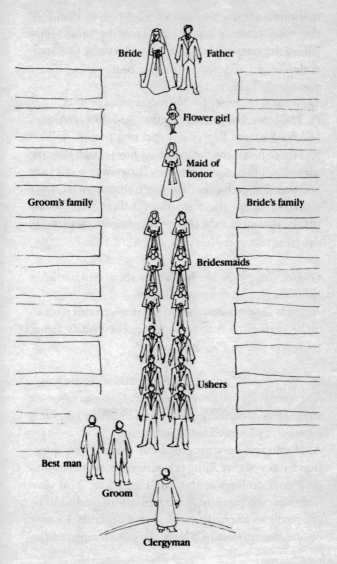

Bride Father

Flower girl

Maid of honor

Groom's family

Bride's family

Bridesmaids

Ushers

Best man

Groom

Clergyman

offending question with a very lovely sentiment. At the appropriate place in the ceremony, he asked, "Who represents the families in blessing this marriage?"

Q. *What is the order for the recessional?*
A. The bride and groom together lead the recessional, followed by the flower girl and ring bearer, walking together. Next are the maid of honor and the best man. The other attendants step forward two at a time and pair off, each usher escorting a bridesmaid down the aisle. When there are more ushers than bridesmaids, the extra men follow the couples, walking in

Bridesmaids   Ushers

Maid of honor   Best man

Flower girl

pairs. If there is an odd man, he walks alone at the end. This is the traditional recessional, although it is acceptable for the wedding party to leave as it entered—bridesmaids together and ushers together—if the bride and groom prefer.

Q. *Is it permissible to have a receiving line at the back of the church after the ceremony?*
A. Yes, if there is to be no reception, or if there are many more guests at the ceremony than there will be at the reception, the bride and groom may stop and greet their guests at the back of the church. This is never done if the majority of those present are going on to the reception. The receiving line, in order, consists of the bride's mother, the bride, the groom and the bridesmaids. The groom's mother certainly may be included, but the fathers need not stand in the line.

Q. *What part do grandparents have in a wedding?*
A. A very special part—they are most honored guests. The grandmothers receive a corsage and they are seated directly behind (or next to, if preferred) the parents during the ceremony and they are seated at the parents' table during the reception.

Q. *Are all Jewish weddings held in synagogues?*
A. Although some Jewish weddings are held in synagogues, they need not be; therefore many are held in hotels, halls or clubs, with the ceremony and the reception in the same place.

Q. Are Orthodox and Conservative ceremonies the same as Reform services?
A. No, they differ in certain aspects. In the first two, the processional is led by the ushers, followed by the bridesmaids. The rabbi comes next, accompanied by the cantor (if one is participating in the ceremony), then the best man and next the groom, walking between his parents. The maid of honor follows them, and the bride, escorted by her parents, comes last.

The ceremony is performed under a canopy called a *chuppah*, sometimes made of flowers but more often a richly decorated cloth. The bride, groom and the two honor attendants stand under

the *chuppah* during the ceremony, as do the parents if it is large enough. Much of the service is conducted in Hebrew.

The bride and groom always lead the recessional. The order of the bridal party may vary, but generally the two sets of parents follow, then the maid of honor with the best man, the rabbi and cantor and finally the bridesmaids and ushers.

The Reform service is usually very similar to a Christian wedding in arrangement. English is used and the canopy may be dispensed with. The groom is ushered by his best man, and the bride is escorted by her father. The order of attendants is the same as in a Christian ceremony. The bride's father, although he

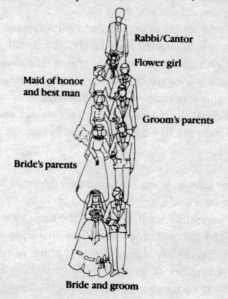

Rabbi/Cantor

Flower girl

Maid of honor
and best man

Groom's parents

Bride's parents

Bride and groom

escorts her, does not give her away in a Jewish ceremony.

Q. *How do Roman Catholic ceremonies differ from Protestant wedding ceremonies?*

A. In marriage ceremonies that include participation in a nuptial mass the bridal party is often seated, with the bride and groom seated on two chairs before the altar. There generally is a kneeling bench, and the maid of honor and the best man remain in the sanctuary with the bride and groom. Guests and members of the wedding party may receive Communion during the mass only if they are Catholic, and, while it is preferred that both the best man and maid of honor be Catholic, at least one must be.

If Communion is served during Protestant ceremonies, which occurs very rarely, the bridal party usually remains standing or is seated to the side as guests come forward to receive the sacrament. Otherwise, the processional, the arrangement of attendants during the ceremony, the recessional and the other details are like those for other Protestant weddings.

Q. *How does a home wedding differ from a traditional church wedding?*

A. The ceremony itself is exactly the same as it is in church and the order for the processional is, too. The only differences are that, unless the home is a mansion, the number of guests and attendants is fewer and there is no recessional. After congratulating you, the clergyman steps aside, an usher removes the prayer bench, if one is used, and your family and friends come forward to offer their best wishes.

Q. *What is the order of the processional, ceremony and recessional for a double wedding?*
A. Both grooms' ushers go first, followed by the bridesmaids and maid of honor of one bride and then that bride and her father. If the two brides are sisters, the older sister and her attendants are the first in the processional. After the first bride and her father, the second bride's bridesmaids follow, then her maid of honor, then the bride and her escort. If the two brides are sisters, the younger sister would be escorted by an older brother or nearest male relative or a close family friend.

During the ceremony, the service is read to both couples, but those points that require responses are read twice. The first, or older, bride and groom answer first.

At the end of the ceremony, the first bride and groom leave first, followed by the second bride and groom. The maids of honor follow, walking with the two best men, then the bridesmaids and ushers, in pairs, with the older couple's attendants going first.

Q. *How else does a double wedding differ from a single wedding?*
A. They don't really differ, other than in the areas mentioned above and in the fact that there are simply more people to arrange. The seating of the parents

during the ceremony is more complicated. When two sisters share a double wedding, both grooms' parents must either agree to share the first pew on the right or they must draw lots for it. If the brides are not sisters, their two mothers share the first pew.

At the reception, two separate receiving lines are formed when the brides are not sisters. When they are sisters, their mother—and their father, if he wishes—stands first. Next to them is the first groom's mother, then the first, or older, bride and her groom, followed by the second groom's mother, and then the second bride and groom. Both maids of honor join the line, but not the bridesmaids since the line is already quite long. If the grooms' fathers wish to be in the receiving line, they would stand after their wives.

When each couple has many attendants, it is better that they have separate bridal tables, close to or facing each other. Each couple has their own cake, and they cut them one after the other so that each may watch the other's ceremony.

If there are three sets of parents involved, they generally share the parents' table at the reception. If four sets of parents are involved, it is more comfortable to have two separate tables so that grandparents, etc., may be included.

Q. *If I wear a veil over my face, when is it turned back and by whom?*
A. Your veil would be turned back by your father, before he leaves your side, or by your maid of honor, before your final vows. You should discuss this with

your minister and go through the motions during your rehearsal so that it is a smooth and graceful process.

Q. When and how do I give my flowers to my maid of honor to hold during the ceremony? When do I take them back again?

A. You give your flowers to your maid of honor after you have turned to face the altar. You retrieve your flowers after you have kissed your groom, as you turn to face your guests in preparation for the recessional.

Q. Does my wedding ring go on my finger over my engagement ring?

A. No, it is always on your finger closest to your heart. This means that while you are dressing you should switch your engagement ring to your right hand so that you don't have to worry about removing it during the ceremony. After your wedding ring has been slipped on your finger you may return your engagement ring to that finger.

Q. I want to wear gloves but don't know if I am supposed to leave them on during the ceremony. Does my wedding ring go on over the gloves?

A. No, it does not. Your wedding ring must be placed on your finger, devoid of other jewelry or gloves. To resolve this, you can do several things. You can remove the gloves, but don't even consider this if you are wearing long, tight gloves, for it will seem to take an eternity to get them off. It is better to wear finger-less gloves so that they may stay on but not present a problem at ring time, or you may open the seam of the ring finger of the left hand glove, for the same reason.

Your Reception

Q. *My reception will be held at my parents' club. The manager has helped with all the arrangements. Do we tip him? If so, how much? Do we tip the chef who made the wedding cake?*

A. The manager of the club would not expect a tip, but if he or she has assisted with the arrangements, then a tip is in order. The size of the tip would depend on the amount of extra effort beyond his usual duties, which he made on your behalf. It might be anything from $25 to over $100. The chef would not expect a tip either, although it would not be unwelcome and might be given for extraordinary accommodation to your wishes; the creation of a beautiful and delicious wedding cake, etc. The tip would be anywhere from $10 to a small percentage of the food bill for the reception. If a tip is not given, and it is not usual for one to be, a thank-you should be extended to the chef, either in person or via the manager.

Q. *Although gratuities for the servers and bartenders are included in the caterer's fee, do I also tip the caterer?*

A. It is not necessary to tip the caterer, as he or she is the owner of the business.

Q. *Can we order a cake from a bakery instead of through the club where the reception will be held?*

A. Yes. Just be sure to make arrangements for the delivery of the cake with the manager and make sure that the cost of ingredients and labor for the cake are not included in your bill for the reception.

Q. *Are there any rules or guidelines about wedding cakes?*
A. No, there are no rules or even guidelines, although wedding cakes are almost always iced and decorated in white. Traditional wedding cakes used to be white fruit cakes, but today they can be any flavor the bride and groom choose, including chocolate. The decorations are most tasteful when they are made from icing. Fresh flowers are a lovely topping to the cake.

Q. *When is the wedding cake cut, and what is the procedure?*
A. At a sit-down reception the cake is cut just before dessert is served. When the reception is a buffet, the cake is cut later, usually shortly before the bride and groom leave.

The bride cuts the first two slices, with the groom helping by placing his hand over hers. He feeds her the first bite and she feeds him the second—but neatly, with no squishing of cake and icing into each other's faces! When the ceremony is completed, a waiter cuts the rest of the cake and others pass it to the guests.

Q. *What is a groom's cake?*
A. One type of groom's cake is a fruit cake. Slices are cut and put into individual white boxes, tied with white satin ribbon and decorated with the combined initials of the bride and groom. These boxes are placed on a table near the door, and each departing guest is expected to take one as a memento of the wedding.

The cost of this tradition has become prohibitive for many people and it has consequently become less prevalent. It is, however, a lovely custom and providing the cake could be a thoughtful and unusual wedding gift (after consulting with the bride) from a family friend who is skilled at baking. When made as a gift, the individual pieces may be wrapped in white paper and tied with white or silver ribbon.

Another type of groom's cake is a chocolate cake that is placed on a separate table from the bride's cake. It is not cut by the couple or served as is the bride's cake, but is sliced by a waiter so that guests who prefer chocolate cake are free to help themselves. The groom's cake, like the bride's cake, is provided by the bride's family.

Q. How do we plan flowers for the hall where the reception will be held?
A. When you meet with the caterer, decorating is one of the topics on your checklist. Often the caterer is able to include flowers in the overall arrangements you make with him or her. If you prefer to supply your own flowers from the florist or your garden, the caterer can recommend what is customarily used to decorate the hall.

Generally, flowers are white, white mixed with colors or pastel shades chosen to blend with the colors of the bridal party or the tablecloths.

A buffet table may have a bowl of flowers for a centerpiece if the cake is not being used. The bridal table usually has a low, centered floral arrangement so the bridal couple is not hidden from the guests, and often one or two more arrangements at each side if the table is long. Candles may be used, too, for an evening or after-dusk reception, but not for a morning or early afternoon reception. Guests' tables generally each have a small floral arrangement.

Other than the flowers on the tables, the only decoration is near or behind the receiving line—either a bank of greens, a fireplace with a bowl of flowers at each end or a stanchion topped with a vase of flowers at each end.

Q. *Who should stand next to whom in the receiving line at my reception?*
A. The bride's mother stands at the head of the line to greet the guests. The groom's mother stands next. If the two fathers are part of the receiving line, which is optional, the father of the bride is second in the line and the father of the groom stands after his wife. Next is the bride, followed by the groom and then the maid of honor. The bridesmaids would be next in line. Their presence is quite correct but is optional and at the discretion of the bride.

At a very large formal wedding there is occasionally an announcer standing next to the bride's mother. He asks the guests their names as they approach and repeats the names to the mother of the bride.

Q. *My parents are divorced. Do they both stand in the receiving line?*
A. Contrary to what many people think, the tradi-

tional receiving line does not include the fathers. So if one set of parents, or both, are divorced, only the mothers of the bride and groom need stand in the receiving line.

Q. *Who sits at the parents' table during the reception?*
A. The mother and father of both the bride and the groom, the grandparents, the clergyman who performs the ceremony and his or her spouse are included. If there is room, godparents, relatives and close family friends are also seated at this table. At large receptions there are sometimes separate parents' tables for the groom's parents and the bride's parents. This is perfectly correct, but not as much in keeping with the symbolism of "joining" that a wedding represents.

Q. *How should my parents, who are divorced, be seated at the reception?*
A. Divorced parents of the bride or groom are never seated together at the parents' table. If they are reasonably friendly, the parent giving the reception will invite the other, but will seat him or her at a separate table. Stepparents are included at the parents' tables, assuming that he or she gets along with the stepchild—the bride or groom. If there has been great bitterness, it is best that the parent who is not giving the wedding, and his spouse, not attend the reception at all even though they go to the marriage ceremony. If the bride or groom insists, the father or mother might come for a short time, but to avoid possible

unpleasantness his or her spouse should tactfully stay away.

Q. Who sits at the table with the bride and groom?
A. When there is a bride's table, the bride and groom sit at the center with the maid of honor on the groom's left and the best man on the bride's right. The other attendants sit on either side. Insofar as possible, men and women alternate. Attendants' husbands, wives and fiancé(e)s should also be seated at the table, and live-in companions are included if there is room. Additionally, siblings of the bride and groom who are not in the wedding party may sit at the bride's table, as may close friends who aren't members of the wedding party. Frequently the bridal party is so large that there is not room at this table for spouses and significant others to be seated at the bride's table. In this case, the bride should make an extra effort to be sure they are seated at tables where they will be comfortable and have a good time.

It is also correct for the bride and groom to circulate among their guests rather than be seated at a bridal table. There should, however, be one reserved table, large enough to seat the attendants, too, so that the bride and groom may always have a place to sit down to eat. In this case, married attendants may be seated at other tables with their spouses, but should be "on call" to gather for the best man's toast and the cutting of the cake as well as to check frequently with the bride and groom to see if there is anything they can do for them.

Q. Do we have to have a master of ceremonies at our wedding?

A. Absolutely not. There has never been a need to have a person at a microphone shouting out directions, introducing the bridal party, announcing the first dance, etc. If there is a band or a disk jockey, the band leader or the disk jockey can make any simple announcements that are required, tastefully and quietly.

Q. I've been at weddings where the band leader or the disk jockey announced the wedding party at the reception. Do we have to do this?

A. I personally deplore the introduction of this component to a reception, primarily because it necessitates that the bride, groom and entire bridal party be separated from the guests during the cocktail hour. They stay in a separate room until guests are seated for the meal to begin and then are brought in, one at a time or a couple at a time, until the bride and groom appear to the announcement, "And now, ladies and gentlemen, appearing for the first time, it's Mr. and Mrs. Jonathan Seidel!" Everyone is to cheer and whistle and clap, and the bride and groom, beaming brightly, dash through the doorway and run lightly to their table. The truth of the matter is that guests would far prefer to have time during the cocktail hour to talk with the members of the wedding party and socialize in a way that becomes restricted once everyone is seated at his or her assigned place.

Q. Should divorced parents appear together in a photograph with the bride and groom?
A. No. Each one should have a picture taken with the couple separately.

Q. Should stepparents be included in the photographs?
A. Yes, if they are on friendly terms with the bride and groom.

Q. After we dance the first dance, what is the order for dancing at the reception?
A. The groom's father usually cuts in on the bride and groom and the groom asks the bride's mother to dance. The bride's father dances with the bride next, the groom's father cuts in on the bride's mother and the groom asks his own mother to dance. The best man usually is fourth to dance with the bride. The precise order is not important so long as each of the principal men dances with the bride and the mothers first. The dancing, after that, becomes general.

Q. I have both a father and a stepfather and am worried about which to choose for a daddy/daughter spotlight dance. Do I have to do this?
A. No you do not have to do this. You should dance with both your father and stepfather, but this can be accomplished quietly and easily, without the need for announcements or having the focus be on you and your two fathers, one at a time. More and more, the traditional order for dancing is being supplanted by a bride-and-groom-only dance, during which they

indicate that their wedding party and then all the guests should begin to dance, too.

Q. Who makes toasts at the reception and when are they made?
A. After the receiving line has disbanded, the bridal party seated and all champagne glasses filled, the best man rises and makes the first toast to the bride and groom. Other members of the bridal party may propose toasts, and the groom generally toasts his bride and his new in-laws.

If there is no bridal table, the attendants form a group when the receiving line finishes and the best man, asking for silence, offers his toast.

Q. What sort of toasts are appropriate?
A. A best man's toast to the bridal couple may be something like: "To Jessica and Michael—may they always be as happy as they look today." The prime ingredient in an appropriate toast is simply that the sentiment be from the heart.

After the best man has made his toast, the groom may propose a toast to his new bride.

Q. Are congratulatory telegrams, faxes or notes read aloud?
A. If telegrams or other messages have been received from invited guests who weren't able to be present, they are read aloud by the best man following the toasts. He then gives the telegrams to the bride's parents for safekeeping until the bride and groom return

from their honeymoon and are able to acknowledge them.

Q. *When does the bride throw the bouquet?*
A. After the cake is cut and before the bride leaves to change her clothes.

Q. *Does my groom have to remove my garter and throw it if I throw a bouquet?*
A. No, and the older the bride the more inappropriate this component is.

Q. *Do I give favors to my wedding guests?*
A. Among many ethnic groups favors are given to all guests at the reception. Whether or not you choose to give them will depend upon tradition within your family. Favors vary from a small, wrapped piece of wedding cake to gold charms!

Q. *We sent a gift to the bride and groom but most people gave money. They stood in line to give their gift and received a favor from the bride. We didn't know what to do since we had no envelope. What should we have done?*
A. The lining up to give gifts of money is seen in a variety of ethnic groups where wedding gifts other than money are seldom given. The purpose is for the bride and groom to thank you for attending their wedding, and to give you a token of their appreciation. It is not a tit for tat exchange of money for favor. This line also is a chance for the guests to bid

farewell to the bride and groom, to wish them well and to depart shortly thereafter. Therefore, you would stand in the line, extend your best wishes and be given a favor not because you handed over an envelope, but because you were an honored guest.

Gifts and Gift Giving

Q. *I've received an invitation to a wedding but not to the reception. Must I send a gift?*
A. No. There is no obligation attached to an invitation to the wedding only, although you may send one if you wish.

Q. *Does a wedding announcement obligate me to send a gift?*
A. No. As with an invitation to the wedding only, the receipt of an announcement does not demand a gift in return. Of course, you may send a gift, but you do not have to.

Q. *How much should be spent on a wedding gift?*
A. There is no "formula" to determine the amount you should spend on a wedding gift. The size or the elaborateness of the wedding should have nothing to do with the amount you spend or give. Your decision should be based on a combination of two things—your affection for the bride, the groom or their families, and your financial capability. No one should ever feel that he must spend more than he can afford. On the other hand, you should spend what you can afford and not give a "piddling" gift to a bride whose family are old friends.

Q. *Friends have asked how checks given as wedding presents should be made out. What do we tell them?*
A. When given before the wedding they are made out to either the bride or to both the bride and groom using her maiden name and his full name—"Meave

Cox and Peter Wadsworth," for example. When given after the wedding, they are made out to the bride and groom—"Meave and Peter Wadsworth"—assuming the bride is changing her name.

Q. *We are planning to give a check as a gift. Do we mail it or take it to the wedding?*
A. If it is customary in your area to give money as a gift, the money is usually brought with you to the reception, although checks may also be sent to the couple before the wedding. With some ethnic groups, as the reception draws to a close, a line generally forms near the bridal table. The guests sometimes receive a small favor or memento of the wedding from the bride and groom as they give them the check. In other cases, there may be a table provided for gifts and envelopes. If you are giving cash, however, never just leave the envelope on a table—hand it directly to the groom or to the bride if she has a receptacle in which to put it.

Q. *How do I know when to give money as a wedding present and when to give a gift?*
A. Whether or not to give money as a wedding present is determined by tradition within your family, ethnic custom, the circumstances of the bride and groom and your own feelings. At one time some people viewed money as either crass or indicating one didn't take time to shop for a gift. Often it was neither, but the ideal vehicle to allow the couple to get exactly what they wanted or to pool their gifts

of money toward a large purchase such as furniture. Close family members may know of a large purchase the couple hopes to make and provide a token gift with a check toward the larger purchase. One woman I know gave her granddaughter a set of sheets to fit a convertible sofa bed, with a check and a note that said she hoped it was delivered by Thanksgiving because she was looking forward to using it!

If a couple is not going to be setting up their own home for some time, because of continuing education, for instance, they may find money more useful than another set of linens to save for that home. If a gift is truly meant to help a couple "get off to a good start," then couples may even elect to use the money to pay off education loans, or for whatever other use they see fit.

Q. *We would like to personalize a gift of linens by having them monogrammed. How should they be marked?*
A. Ashley Elizabeth Hopewell, who will marry George Thomas Simpson, could have linen embroidered with her married initials:

$$\mathcal{AS} \qquad \text{or} \qquad \mathcal{ASH}$$

or with her future husband's last initial:

$$\mathcal{S}$$

When a bride chooses to keep her own name after marriage, the two last initials are used with a decorative device between:

Naturally, linen that is monogrammed before an engagement is marked with the bride's maiden initials.

Q. *Where are square linens marked; rectangular ones?*
A. Square tablecloths are marked in one corner midway between center and corner so that the monogram shows on the table.

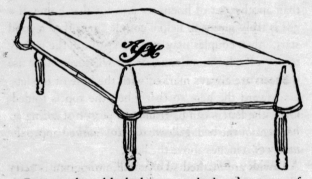

Rectangular tablecloths are marked at the center of each long side midway between the table edge and the center of the cloth.

Very large damask napkins are marked in the center of one side, smaller ones in the corner—usually diagonally, but sometimes straight. To determine the best place to monogram napkins, fold one exactly as it will be folded for use and then make a light pencil outline in the center of the fold.

Sheets are always marked with the base of the letters toward the hem so that when the top is folded down, the letters can be read by a person standing at the front of the bed. Pillowcases are marked approximately two inches above the hem.

Towels are marked so that the monogram is centered when the towels are folded in thirds and hung on the rack.

Q. *If we are able to give my niece and future nephew everyday dishes, we would like to, but don't know what the basic requirements would be. Is there a guideline for what is needed in the way of everyday dishes?*

A. Usually, a complete set of four or six place settings of inexpensive china, stoneware, pottery or unbreakable plastic ware serves nicely as everyday dishes. It generally includes:

> Dinner plates
> Dessert plates (which do double duty as salad plates)
> Cereal dishes (used also for soup, puddings, fruit, etc.)
> Mugs or cups
> Saucers if cups are chosen
> Cream pitcher and sugar bowl
> Optional: two platters and two vegetable dishes

Q. *What does a typical place setting consist of?*
A. Dishes for entertaining include:

> Soup cup (two-handled, for both clear and cream soups)
> Dinner plate
> Salad plate (may double as a dessert plate)
> Bread and butter plate
> Cup
> Saucer
> Optional: cream soup plates, demitasse cups

Additional options are not a part of the individual place setting but do complete a set of china:

> Cream pitcher and sugar bowl
> Platters and vegetable dishes

Gravy boat
Sauce bowls for hollandaise, mayonnaise, etc.

Q. *A group of us is giving a gift together of a few place settings of the bride's chosen silver flatware pattern. How should this flatware be monogrammed?*
A. Either a single letter—the initial of the groom's last name—or a triangle of letters is used for monogramming flatware. If the triangle of block letters is used, there are three variations that may be considered:

The last-name initial may go below with the first-name initials of the bride and groom above. When Samantha Adams Burns marries Henry Wilson Carter:

The flatware may be engraved with the bride's married initials:

Or with the last-name initial above and their two first-name initials below:

If a man is a "Junior," the "Jr." is not used when the initials form a design, as on flat silver.

Any initialing should be simple in style. Elongated Roman goes well on modern silver, and Old English is best on the more ornamented styles. Monograms have always been placed so that the top of the letter is toward the end of the handle. It appears upside down as seen by the diner at that place. Although this is traditional, it is acceptable to reverse the direction so that the initials are legible to the user, if you prefer.

Q. *Where are wedding gifts sent—to the bride's home or to her parents' home?*
A. Gifts are usually sent to the bride's home before the day of the wedding, addressed to her in her maiden name. When they are sent after the wedding takes place, they go to the bride and groom at their new address or in care of the bride's family.

Q. *My best buddy is getting married. May I send my gift to his home?*
A. You seldom send a present to the bridegroom. Even though he is your closest friend and you may never have met his bride, your present is sent to her—unless you send two presents, one in courtesy to her and one in affection to him. More often, friends of the bridegroom do pick out things suitable for him, such as a decanter or masculine desk accessories, which are sent to her but are obviously intended for his use.

Q. *May duplicate wedding presents be exchanged?*
A. Yes. Whether or not you inform the donor of your action is entirely up to you.

Q. *Should wedding presents be displayed? Where should they be displayed? Should cards showing the names of the donors be displayed with them?*

A. Wedding gifts certainly may be displayed, if you wish. Gifts should be displayed at home only, never in a hotel, club or catering facility. Whether or not you display cards with them is a matter of personal preference. Although many people like to know who gave the present, others feel that publicizing this information invites comparisons that may be embarrassing.

Q. *How should checks be displayed?*
A. They should be arranged overlapping, so that the signature but not the amount shows. Cover them with a piece of glass to keep them in place.

Q. *When a wedding gift arrives broken, what should we do?*
A. Take it back to the store from which it came without mentioning the fact to the donor. However, if it has arrived directly through the mail and the package is insured, the donor should be notified so that he or she can collect insurance.

Q. *Have you any suggestions for keeping track of wedding gifts?*
A. Yes. In order to keep your gifts organized, to know who gave what and where it came from in case of exchanges, and whether or not a thank-you has been sent, a gift list is a necessity. Obtain sheets of numbered stickers (or plain ones on which you can write a number) and affix one sticker in the "gift number" column and one with a corresponding num-

ber on the bottom of the gift. Do it as you open each gift so there will be no possibility of confusion. You can make your own notebook of pages, or you can purchase a book designed for this purpose that may come with sheets of numbered stickers. A sticker goes on only one item of a set—one of a dozen plates, for example.

gift no.	description	sent by	date rcd.	sender's address	where purchased	thank-you sent
6	8 glass plates	Mrs. Green	4/12	Louden Dr. Rye, NY 10580	Bloomingdale's	4/14

Q. *When should thank-you notes be sent?*
A. The wise bride writes her notes on the day the gift arrives for as long as she can, both as a courtesy to the sender and to keep herself from becoming inundated with notes to write after the honeymoon. In ordinary circumstances, all thank-you notes should be sent within three months of the date of the wedding.

Q. *Are thank-you notes signed by both the bride and the groom?*
A. It is not incorrect to sign both of your names. It is preferable for one to sign with a reference in the text to the other, such as "John and I both thank you for..." to make clear you both appreciate the gift. Another way for the bride or groom to include the other is to close the note "With love from both of us, Betsy Ann."

Q. *Does the groom write any of the thank-you notes?*
A. Since most wedding gifts are sent to the bride, she usually writes and signs the thank-you note. But there is no reason the groom should not share this task. I'm sure there are many relatives and friends of the groom who would be delighted to receive a thank-you note from him rather than from a bride who is a relative stranger to them.

Q. *Are printed thank-you cards an acceptable way of acknowledging wedding presents?*
A. No. Every present must be acknowledged by a personal handwritten note. Even if a printed thank-you card incorporating the bridal couple's wedding picture is used, there must always be a personal hand-written message included.

Q. *Should wedding presents be opened at the reception?*
A. At a small wedding where there are only a few, they may be opened, but if there are many presents, it is better to wait until later so that the bride and groom may mingle with the guests. The couple will also appreciate the gifts more if they open them at their leisure.

Index

About the Author

Elizabeth L. Post, granddaughter-in-law of the legendary Emily Post, has earned the mantle of her predecessor as America's foremost authority on etiquette. Mrs. Post has revised the classic *Etiquette* five times since 1965. In addition she has written *Emily Post's Complete Book of Wedding Etiquette*, *Emily Post's Wedding Planner*, *Emily Post's Advice for Every Dining Occasion*, *Emily Post on Business Etiquette*, *Emily Post on Entertaining*, *Emily Post on Etiquette*, *Emily Post on Guests and Hosts*, *Emily Post on Invitations*, *Emily Post on Second Weddings*, *Please, Say Please*, *The Complete Book of Entertaining* with co-author Anthony Staffieri, and *Emily Post Talks with Teens about Manners and Etiquette* with co-author Joan M. Coles. Mrs. Post's advice on etiquette may also be found in the monthly column she writes for *Good Housekeeping* magazine, "Etiquette for Everyday."

Mrs. Post and her husband divide their time between homes in Florida and Vermont.